THE BOSTONER REBBETZIN *Remembers*

Rebbetzin Raichel Horowitz of Boston/Har Nof recalls Jewish life in Poland, America and Israel

Published by
Mesorah Publications, ltd

R.O.F.E.H. International
Special Edition . . . November 1996

Published and Distributed by
MESORAH PUBLICATIONS, Ltd.
4401 Second Avenue
Brooklyn, New York 11232

Distributed in Europe by
J. LEHMANN HEBREW BOOKSELLERS
20 Cambridge Terrace
Gateshead, Tyne and Wear
England NE8 1RP

Distributed in Israel by
SIFRIATI / A. GITLER—BOOKS
4 Bilu Street
P.O.B. 14075
Tel Aviv 61140

Distributed in Australia & New Zealand by
GOLD'S BOOK & GIFT CO.
36 William Street
Balaclava 3183, Vic., Australia

Distributed in South Africa by
KOLLEL BOOKSHOP
22 Muller Street
Yeoville 2198, Johannesburg, South Africa

ARTSCROLL HISTORY SERIES®
THE BOSTONER REBBETZIN REMEMBERS

ISBN
0-89906-592-9 (hard cover)
0-89906-593-7 (paperback)

Typography by Compuscribe at ArtScroll Studios, Ltd.

Printed in the United States of America by Noble Book Press Corp.
Bound by Sefercraft, Quality Bookbinders, Ltd. Brooklyn, N.Y.

MOSDOS BOSTON
under the spiritual leadership of

GRAND RABBI LEVI YITZCHOK HOROWITZ
the Bostoner Rebbe, Shlita
of Boston – Har Nof

is proud of its contributions to the general welfare of the Jewish people throughout the world, and its many projects effecting the spiritual and physical betterment of Klal Yisroel. These include:

1) The New England Chassidic Center – Congregation Beth Pinchas (the Rebbe's personal Shul), which has served Boston's traditional community for more than 50 years.
2) The Out-Reach and Shabbaton programs that have touched the lives of thousands, many of whom have become Baalei T'shuvah, with a large number subsequently settling in Eretz Yisrael.
3) Kollel Boston in Har Nof – Launched 20 years ago, it was the first post-graduate rabbinical school to serve married Baalei T'shuvah.
4) Pioneering in the founding of the Har Nof community in Jerusalem – now a famous landmark of Torah and Chassidus with the Rebbe's Tish, a highlight for the many privileged to attend.
5) Talmud Torah – Boston in Jerusalem and Bnei Brak, with an enrollment of close to 300 children in a very short period of time, serving the Anglo Saxon community in addressing its special needs.
6) Beis Medrash – Givat Pinchas of Har Nof, where thousands of individuals Daven and learn daily, from the crack of dawn to midnight, as well as the Beis Shlomo Boston Shul of Har Nof South and the Kiryat Sefer Bostoner Shul.
7) The men's Mikvaos in the Boston and Har Nof Shuls, enabling hundreds of men to elevate the spiritual intensity of their Davening.

and finally . . .

8) The special jewel in the Rebbe's crown ROFEH International, the world-renowned health organization, which saved hundreds of lives throughout its efforts during the last 40 years.

R.O.F.E.H. INTERNATIONAL

Reaching **O**ut **F**urnishing **E**mergency **H**ealthcare

ROFEH ☐ An international medical referral center helping patients from all over the world

ROFEH ☐ A service run under the auspices of the renowned Bostoner Rebbe, Shlita, meeting the Halachic and ethical challenges of modern medicine and responding to the call of human suffering

ROFEH ☐ A unique organization providing FREE long – and short – term housing to outpatients and their companions

ROFEH ☐ A non-profit agency offering FREE support services, transportation, counseling and interpretation

ROFEH ☐ A humanitarian operation widely acclaimed for its Chesed and unparalleled benevolence

ROFEH ☐ Where patients can turn for medical, psychological, spiritual and emotional guidance

ROFEH ☐ A home away from home, where patients find comfort, compassion and camaraderie

ROFEH ☐ A Jewish lifesaving endeavor, symbolizing hope, courage, solace and trust

JOIN ROFEH – SHARE IN THE MITZVAH OF CHESED.

EXTEND A HELPING HAND TODAY – SAVE A JEWISH LIFE.

This book is dedicated
to the memory of
my beloved and saintly parents z"l
who serve as an inspiration to me
and my children

❧ ❧ ❧

And to my dear and special friend
Blanche Goldman
of Brookline, MA and Las Vegas, NV
a true Eiyshes Chayil,
and the entire Goldman Family,
who are unique in their chessed.

Table of Contents

Foreword

In these days, when so many young Jewish women are searching for their roots and for authentic role models, this book seems particularly important and timely. There are few books like it, for it is a book by a very special woman, about a very special woman and for very special women. Filled with a love of *Yiddishkeit*, life and others, it flows straight from heart to heart.

My admiration for its author and her *chessed*, dedication and determination is in no way diminished by the fact that she is my own Rebbetzin. On the contrary, I am all the more aware of her many unrecorded virtues and accomplishments. I can only hope that her book will inspire others, as she has inspired me.

Grand Rabbi Levi Y. Horowitz

Acknowledgments

My heart is full of gratitude to *HaKadosh Baruch Hu,* Who, through His great kindness, gave me the *zechus* to see so much, to do so much and to help so many people. I am also grateful to my husband, the Rebbe, *Shlita,* who shared this life and these stories with me, and who encouraged me to write them down for our children, grandchildren and great-grandchildren.

On a more practical level, I wish to thank Mrs. Sarah Mushka Honig who taped and transcribed our lengthy series of interviews, and helped organize them chronologically. I greatly value the many hours we spent together on this project. I also wish to thank Dr. I. M. Asher who helped me edit this material and put it into book form, adding explanatory and transitional material as necessary, while preserving its direct style. Special thanks are due to

Mrs. Adele Asher, who undertook the massive task of typing and proofreading draft after draft of her husband's manuscript.

Last, but far from least, I wish to thank Rabbi Meir Zlotowitz, Rabbi Nosson Scherman and their talented ArtScroll staff for making this book such a beautiful and satisfying reality. I particularly appreciate their letting me tell my story in my own way, without limiting me unduly to the style manual and grammar book. The resulting words come truly from the heart. To them all, my thanks.

Finally, I have undergone many trials in my life, some small, some more serious. I have reported them as I felt them personally at the time. Obviously only Hashem can look into the hearts of others or see their actions and motivations in their true broader context. I have tried to be careful, and have left far more stories untold than told. Still, if I have misjudged or offended anyone, that was certainly not my intention. Rather, my sharing my reactions to these events had but one purpose: to let you know that, while life may contain certain disappointments, difficulties and even betrayals, this must not affect your love of people and your determination to help them. This is true *chessed* and the story that I wanted to tell.

Introduction

Perhaps I should start at the beginning. Rabbi Yisrael Baal Shem Tov started the Chassidic movement over 250 years ago. He emphasized living according to Torah, living with joy and loving all Jews. A Chassidic community is like a family, and Jews from all over come to a Rebbe not only for religious advice, but also for personal, psychological, business, medical and any and all other types of advice. A Rebbe's door is always open and every Jew, religious or not, must be helped.

A Rebbetzin's job is also to help, listen and support. Every year, several thousand Jews — Torah scholars, college students, businessmen, beggars, saints and perhaps even a few scoundrels — pass through our winter home at the New England Chassidic Center in Boston and our summer home in Jerusalem. Although the weather would dictate the opposite, we do it this way because our job is to be where we are needed most, when we are needed most.

Meeting so many different types of people, a Rebbetzin naturally has a head full of memories and stories. I remember, for example, the time during the '60s when the Rebbe's secretary ran in to tell me there was an offbeat young man downstairs. He claimed to be the *Mashiach* (Messiah) and wanted to see the Rebbe at once. What should she do? I told her to just send him to me in the kitchen — he was the third "*Mashiach*" to drop by that week! I made him some coffee, and we talked things over a bit and he calmed down.

Where does a Rebbetzin tell her stories? Sometimes when she leads the women's *tish* on Friday nights or at *Shalosh Seudos,* the third Sabbath meal. Sometimes when she meets her friends and neighbors on a visit, or just waiting for the elevator. In short, anywhere good people get together and feel relaxed. My favorite place, as you may have guessed, is in my kitchen or dining-room table over a cup of coffee. That makes it difficult to preserve the fragile, informal atmosphere of these stories in a book. A "literary" book with lots of footnotes and fancy words would never do. That's why I am so grateful to ArtScroll, our publishers, for agreeing to let me tell my story in my own words. Hopefully, whatever I may lose in rhetoric or grammar will be more than made up for by simplicity and sincerity. A story has to go from heart to heart. With us, this is more than a matter of style; it is a way of life. We Bostoner *Chassidim* try to avoid being pretentious — with others, with ourselves and with G-d.

Why, then, write a book at all? Because I want you and my grandchildren to know how different our world was from the world you see around you. In America, for example, outside of New York, there were almost no kosher foods, *yeshivos* or religious communities. Except for a narrow circle of European immigrants, there was no concept of a Rebbe, and the idea of establishing a native American *Chassidus,* led by an American-born Rebbe, seemed a contradiction in terms. I want you and my grandchildren to understand the struggles we faced day after day. To do so, you must follow me into my world. We will take a leisurely journey through my life, not for any dramatic arrival, but for what we will see along the way.

What we will see, mostly, is not the outside of Boston *Chassidus,* but its inside: the path of *chessed* that the Rebbe and I learned from our parents and have tried to pass on to our children. To me, *chessed* does not mean doing impressive things for others in the full glare of publicity. It means submerging your own emotions and needs to help others, in solitude, without hope of thanks, because you know that others need you and that *Rachmana liba baie,* that G-d desires the heart. If you can achieve that, the rest will take care of itself. In fact, with enough love and effort, even the world of the small and the commonplace can be made holy.

Once I started writing a book, I found that it was no small task. So I decided to keep it simple. We will pretend that you just walked into my kitchen, and that I have just made us a cup of coffee or tea. There's a bit of cake, perhaps left over from Shabbos, and maybe some dried fruit as well. We will start to talk together, you and I. You will tell me some of your stories and then I will tell you some of mine. Or perhaps I should start ....

ONE

Stryzov

Memories

My earliest memories are of Stryzov, a small town in Poland, the "Old Country" for many Jews before the War. There was a water pump in the middle of the town square where people used to gather. Every day someone — often a public water carrier or the family's gentile maid — had to come and pump water. Then they had to haul it back home and pour it into a big water barrel. That was our water supply for the day. I remember, when I was a little girl, going over to our water barrel and looking at my face, mirrored deep inside. This is my earliest memory, and a symbolic one at that — deep down, we always see ourselves, wherever we look in this world.

Across from the water pump was the town *shul*. It was two stories high and, all across the ceiling, an artist had painted a beautiful mural of the Livyasan, the huge fish that will be served at the feast of the *Moshiach,* in the Time to Come. In the summer of 1991, I went back to visit Stryzov. The Jews are gone now; my family and friends were all killed by the Nazis in the Holocaust. The *shul* building is miraculously still standing; but there are no men in black *kapotes* and white *tallaisim davening* inside. Nor are there crowds of *frum* women, dressed in their beautiful white Shabbos clothes, filling the women's galley. The Stryzover *shul* is now a State Library.

As a child, I lived with my grandfather, Reb Alter Ze'ev, the Stryzover Zeide, a great tzaddik and the great-grandson of Reb Naftali of Ropshitz

I remember how my grandfather, Reb Alter Ze'ev, the Stryzover Rav, used to give his *drashas* (sermons) from the *bimah* of the *shul*. My mother told me that I once heard him give a *drasha* to the women of the town on *tznius* (modesty). It must have made quite an impression on me, because, although I was only three years old, I began to be very careful about always buttoning the top button of my blouse!

The mural of the Livyasan is still there on the ceiling; but the *goyim* reading their books and newpapers below have no idea what he represents. He has seen a lot, that old Livyasan. He is full of memories now; and so am I.

At Home

Mother, my older sister Leah and I lived with my grandparents, Reb Alter Ze'ev and Bobeh Yehudis. Bobeh

Yehudis' father, Reb Sender Kalonimus, was a very wealthy man, who owned half the town of Melitz. In fact, as a girl, Bobeh had a private maid and a piano — both quite unusual in those days. When Bobeh got married, she brought my grandfather a large *naddan* (dowry), and with it they had built a roomy four-story house, with extra apartments in the back and a winery and a candy store in front. At that time, there was no electricity in Stryzov, so we used kerosene lamps to light the house. Behind the house there was a large garden with all kinds of vegetables and sunflower seeds which we children used to pick. Beyond it there was a river where we went swimming in the summertime. We used to wear loose housecoats, so we would be modestly dressed, and I still remember how refreshing the cool water felt during the hot summer afternoons.

The basement was rented to a bakery that sold delicious fresh loaves of bread and soft Polish bagels. I remember the smell of that hot bread and the smell of the carnations my mother's friend used to bring us from her garden. To this day, whenever I smell carnations, I still remember this friend and my family in Stryzov.

In the summer we used to buy *pozhenkes*, small, pale wild strawberries that grew in the woods. And all year long we used to get the most marvelous fresh butter from Jewish farmers who lived near the town. The butter, delivered on a large green leaf, was decorated with fancy designs. It's funny how little things like that make such a lasting impression: the beautiful yellow-white butter on its bright green leaf.

Togetherness

Reb Alter Ze'ev and Bobeh Yehudis had eight daughters and one son; and each family had separate apartments in the house. That way the married daughters could be with Bobeh Yehudis, while the sons-in-law learned with Reb Alter Ze'ev. These sons-in-law all turned out to be great *Rabbanim* and *tzaddikim*.

We children had a playroom next to the kitchen, where we were supervised by our very own nursemaid. My favorite toys were a big pan and a wooden spoon, which I would bang together to make a tremendous racket. We would all sing songs and play together. It was wonderful! We were all very close and kind to each other. For example, in those days, there were no such thing as lollipops. Instead, we had brightly colored hard candies shaped like fish. Every day I used to save my own fish candy until my sister Leah came home from school. I wanted to give her some first because I loved her.

The Stryzover Zeide

Reb Alter Ze'ev, the Stryzover Zeide, was the great-grandson of the Ropshitzer Rav. He was a saintly and scholarly man, who was already recognized as an *ilui* (genius) by the age of seven. At seven, he and Bobeh Yehudis became engaged and, when he turned 14, they married. As an adult, Reb Alter Ze'ev fasted all day long. He had his "breakfast" at *Minchah* time, and he wouldn't eat his second meal until midnight. He spent most of his time learning and slept only three hours or so a night.

I remember him well. He had a beautiful sweet voice, like the famous *chazan* Yossele Rosenblatt. I especially remember his Friday night *Kiddush*. He also used to compose his own *nigunim*. Often when the Belzer Rav visited Zeshov (in Yiddish, Reisha), a larger town not far away by train, Reb Alter Ze'ev would travel there for Shabbos to be with him. The Belzer Rebbe would ask Zeide to *daven*, announcing "As a treat for the Reisher *baalabatim*, I call the Stryzover Rav to the *amud*."

The Three Overcoats

They tell an interesting story about Reb Alter Ze'ev's *tzedakah*. When he married my grandmother, his wedding gifts included an impressive wardrobe with three fur *shtreimlach* (fur hats) and three *rozhevilkes*, the beautiful fur-lined silk coats worn by Chassidic Rebbes.

The three *shtreimlach* were to be worn as follows: one only on Shabbos, one only on *Yom Tov* and one, the least expensive, in the rain. Each of the fur-lined silk coats also had its intended use: one was for Shabbos, one was for *Yom Tov* and one was for weekday use. A fur-lined coat was actually a necessity in those days, because the indoor heating in Stryzov was far from efficient. It consisted of a tile-covered oven heated by a wood-burning fire. A person sitting right beside the oven felt warm but, even a short distance away, it was quite cold.

Soon after their wedding, Bobeh Yehudis noticed that one of my grandfathers fur-lined coats had disappeared. She searched high and low for it, but it was nowhere to be found. Finally, she asked Reb Alter Ze'ev if he knew what had happened to the third *rozhevilke.* "Please don't bother looking for it," he told her. "I gave it away to a poor *chassan* who was about to be married. I said to myself: Why should I have three coats, while someone else doesn't even have one?"

Bobeh Yehudis

Bobeh Yehudis' attitude towards *chessed* was much the same. Whenever she had a dress or a pair of shoes made, she would order an extra one and give it away to a poor woman. After a while, she learned that the poor women who received her dresses and shoes felt embarrassed, because people recognized their clothes as part of the Rebbetzin's *tzedakah;* so Grandmother Yehudis changed her tactics. She began giving poor people the same amount of money that it cost to make her own clothes. Then they could buy whatever they wanted, without anyone knowing about it.

Whenever someone in Stryzov was poor or ill and could not prepare their own meals, Bobeh Yehudis would cook huge pots of extra food, and send her daughters over with hot meals for them. My mother, as a young girl of eight or nine, often got burns and bruises from taking those hot pots of soup to the homes of needy people.

The Stryzover Kinder

Bobeh Yehudis first had two girls, Aunt Chana and Aunt Zipporah, and then a boy, Uncle Chaim Yehudah. He and his third wife both perished in the *Churban* (Holocaust). His son, Klonimus Kalman, took over the Stryzov *Rabbanus* a year before Reb Alter Ze'ev was *niftar* (1930). He also perished in the *Churban*.

The night before her son's *bris,* while the *Chassidim* held the customary *vachtnacht,* Bobeh Yehudis dreamt that two very special guests came to the *bris*: Reb Chaim Sanzer, the first Sanzer Rav, and her uncle Reb Yehudah Melitzer. When she woke up, she felt strongly that her son should carry the names of the two great rabbis of her dream: Chaim and Yehudah. However, their family tradition was that Reb Avraham Sendyszover, her father-in-law, should choose the baby's names. Bobeh Yehudis did not tell her father-in-law about her dream but, when people came to wish her a *"Mazal Tov"* after the *bris,* she learned that Reb Avraham himself had named the boy Chaim Yehudah!

After Uncle Chaim Yehudah, Bobeh Yehudis gave birth to two boys; but they both died, since she did not have enough milk to nurse them properly. In those days, baby formula was not available; so when mothers didn't have enough milk, and no Jewish wet-nurses were available, their babies often died of starvation. Her next two daughters were Aunt Brucha and my mother, Rochma Miril.

When my mother was born in 1894, Bobeh Yehudis once again could not find a Jewish wet-nurse. This time she went to the Shinover Rav, the son of the Sanzer Rav, to ask if she could allow a non-Jewish woman to nurse her baby. The Shinover Rav permitted it; and my mother survived. After that, Bobeh Yehudis had four more daughters: Malke, Rochel, Fraide and Tirzah.

The Stryzover's Brachos

Reb Alter Ze'ev accepted *kvitlach* and gave people *brachos,* like any other Chassidic Rebbe. Once a couple who had been childless for years came and asked him for a *brachah.* He promised them a child, if they would give generously to the town's *hachnasas kallah* charity fund, which helped needy brides. They did, and soon they had a child. Another *Chassid* asked for a *brachah* to win the lottery. My grandfather passed away, however, before the lots were drawn. On the day of the lottery, this *Chassid* went to Reb Alter Ze'ev's grave and *davened* there with all his heart. Sure enough, his ticket won, and he was able to pay off his debts and marry off his daughter.

Zeide also learned things from dreams. One night a townsman who had passed away appeared to him in a dream and asked him to learn *mishnayos* in his memory because that night was his *yahrzeit.* Zeide was surprised, since he had not received the usual reminder from the town's Chevra Mishnayos. Bobeh Yehudis woke up all the children, but no one remembered receiving any note. Finally they woke up the Jewish maid, who remembered that she had indeed received just such a note but had forgotten to give it to Reb Alter Ze'ev.

Aunt Bina

Bobeh Yehudis' older sister, Aunt Bina, was a wise and charitable woman. When she and her husband still had no children after a number of years, she went to Rav Meir'l Dzikover, my great-great-grandfather from my father's side, to ask for a *brachah.* Now one of the Dzikover Rav's sons, Reb Naftali Chaim, had moved to *Eretz Yisrael,* where he suffered severe hardships. He wrote to Aunt Bina that if she would send him 90 gold coins, in the merit of her charity, she would have a child within a year.

Aunt Bina gave her husband 90 gold coins to send to Reb Naftali Chaim by mail and soon she was expecting a child. Mysteriously, the money never arrived in *Eretz Yisrael.* Reb Naftali Chaim wrote to Aunt Bina to share his concern that, since her *tzedakah* money had not arrived, the baby's life might be in danger. Unfortunately it was and the baby died. Aunt Bina immediately launched an investigation to find out what had happened to the missing money. She learned that her husband had never sent the coins; instead, he had apparently gambled the money away. She was so beside herself with grief that she decided to seek a divorce. The Dzikover Rav himself tried to make *shalom;* but finally, after Aunt Bina spoke with him privately, he agreed to her divorce.

Despite her deep disappointment, Aunt Bina was always careful about the laws of *lashon hara.* When her friends and relatives would ask her why she wanted a divorce, she would say, "My husband is still my husband, and I can't speak *lashon hara* against him." Later, after the breakup, when her friends and relatives would ask her, she would say, "What! You want me to speak *lashon hara* about a stranger!"

Eventually, Aunt Bina remarried. Her second husband was a widower with eleven children; she raised them all as if they were her own. One became the Rav of Yaslow, which is a town near Stryzov. Mother told me that Aunt Bina was a great *tzadekes* who always gave needy travelers money and baked goods, so they wouldn't go hungry on their journeys.

Mother Goes to Cheder

My mother's oldest sister, Aunt Chana, gave birth to a son, Shloime. He loved all the attention he got as the first grandchild in the family and balked at the notion of going off to *cheder* (grade school) at the ripe old age of three. He wanted to stay at home and play with my mother, five-year-old Rochma Miril.

Zeide suggested that Mother take Shloime to *cheder,* and then he agreed to go. She used to wait for him in the back of the *cheder,* and quickly picked up all the *Chumash* and *davening* that was taught to the little boys there. In those days, however, a girl did not learn such things. When Reb Alter Ze'ev discovered that Mother was now a full-time *"cheder bachur,"* he told Shloime that he was now old enough to go to *cheder* on his own. Mother sat down under the table and cried, "I want to learn too!" Her father explained that *cheder* was not for girls; but that she could read the *Tz'enah U'Renah* instead. Unfortunately, that *sefer,* although it is written in Yiddish, was too hard for her at that age.

Mother did eventually learn to read and write Yiddish. She also studied Polish and German at home until she knew both languages fluently. At that time Galicia, although part of Poland, was under the rule of the German-speaking Kaiser Franz Josef of Austria, and both languages were important. When she was 12, Mother took a correspondence course in Hebrew; and this finally allowed her to read *sefarim* on her own. She read a great deal and eventually became extremely learned. In fact, her Torah insights were often quoted by others.

Moderation

Zeide did teach my mother a lot of other important things, however, in his quiet, patient way. For example, one hot summer day when Mother was only about nine, a poor man came to the house and asked her for breakfast. She put together a beautiful spread. She ran downstairs to the bakery for soft Polish bagels and carried them up to the dining room. She then marched from the kitchen to the dining room several times, each time carrying a different dish: fresh butter, cheese and herring. After the guest had left, the nine-year-old hostess collapsed, exhausted from all her efforts.

Reb Alter Ze'ev noticed all this, and took her quietly aside. *"Hachnasas orchim* is an important *mitzvah,"* he said, "but do you think this man eats such an elaborate breakfast at home?" "No," she answered. "He couldn't afford it." "Hmm, and do you eat so well yourself?" "No," she said, "I can't eat so much." "Hmm, and could you serve another guest right now?" She slowly shook her little head no.

"Well, then," he explained, "if you really want to fulfill the *mitzvah* of *hachnasas orchim,* set the table with a normal breakfast, but don't make it too elaborate. That way, when the next guest arrives, you won't be too tired to take care of him as well."

My Parents' Marriage

In 1910, a match was proposed between my mother, Rochma Miril Horowitz, and my father, Rav Naftali Ungar. My father's mother, Rebbetzin Leah, and Rav Alter Ze'ev were very much in favor of the *shidduch;* but Mother herself was reluctant. Finally she agreed, and the wedding date was set. Sadly, Grandmother Leah died shortly before the wedding. My mother was 16 when she married, and a year later she gave birth to my older sister Leah, who was named after our grandmother. Seven years later, when Mother was already a "matron" of 24, I was born.

Even in Galicia not all marriages worked out and, when I was about four years old, my parents divorced. I vaguely remember my father. Most of the time, we lived with Reb Alter Ze'ev and his family.

Sickness Strikes

In those days, health care was limited at best. Sickness was common and often serious. When Mother was 27, she and my sister Leah came down with typhus. Mother was so ill that she became delirious. She dreamed that she was going to America and she began screaming, "No! I don't want to go to America! I want to stay here!" America, at that time, was no place to live a fully religious life; but her dream did eventually come true.

My sister Leah was very sick too, and her beautiful light-brown hair fell out. She began crying and, although I was only three, I tried to comfort her. I told her that her lovely hair would grow back "like a rose." Although I was often sick, I didn't get typhus. It was a miracle I didn't get typhus.

Mother used to cry over me, because I was so frail and sickly. She once asked Reb Alter Ze'ev what to do about me, but he just smiled and told her not to worry. He said I would live to be an old woman, because I had such a happy-go-lucky nature.

A Lost World

I have much more to say about my childhood, about my grandparents and about Stryzov. Everything about that time, about that world, every detail is precious to me. My family and friends are all gone now, but my memory tries to save every bit it can. Perhaps that is why I use so many Yiddish words in my stories. They too are a part of that world, like the hot Shabbos *challos,* my cousins, and the water pump.

On Shavuos night, 22 years ago, I had a dream. Reb Klonimus Kalman, Reb Alter Ze'ev's grandson and successor, had come back. He told me that he was holding a *Yizkor* service for all those *Yidden,* a whole Europe full of Jews, who had been killed in the *Churban* (Holocaust). When I woke up, I remembered that Rav Kalman himself had died in the *Churban* without children and, from then on, I have always remembered him when saying the *Yizkor* prayers. There is little we can do about the Holocaust and that lost world, but we can try to remember. They are not truly gone, as long as we can tell their story.

TWO

Roots

On Chassidus

To understand my parents and grandparents who were, on both sides, Chassidic Rebbes and Rebbetzins, you first need to know something about *Chassidus* and what it meant to the Jews of Eastern Europe. The Chassidic path to serving Hashem was revealed over 250 years ago in the Ukraine by Rabbi Yisroel Baal Shem Tov. It became a major movement throughout Poland, Hungary and Russia under the leadership of his *talmid,* Reb Dov Ber, the Maggid of Mezritch.

The Maggid's *talmidim* were all great *tzaddikim* and *Rebbeim* in their own right: Reb Levi Yitzchak of Berditchev, Reb Shneur Zalman of Liadi, Reb Shmuel Shmelke of Nikolsburg and his brother, Reb Pinchas HaLevi Horowitz of Frankfurt, Reb Zusia of Hanopoli and his brother, Reb Elimelech (Melech) of Lizhensk. The "Rebbe Reb Melech," as he was called, and his *talmid,* the Chozeh of Lublin, became the teachers of all the great Chassidic Rebbes of

Our son, Reb Mayer, praying at the kever of the Rebbe Reb Elimelech of Lizhensk, one of the founders of Chassidus in Poland

Poland. The Rebbe and I are related to many of them, as you can see on the family tree at the end of this book. The Rebbe is the seventh-generation grandson of Reb Shmuel Shmelke.

The Maggid's *talmidim* were all quite different personalities and each developed his own unique kind of *Chassidus.* What they had in common was a burning devotion to the *Ribono Shel Olam* (Master of the World) and His Torah, a deep love for all Jews and a willingness to go far beyond the call of duty in helping their fellow man.

Most people in America today have no idea of what a Chassidic Rebbe used to be. In Europe, the Rebbe was everything to his followers: a teacher, a judge, a father, a leader, an advisor and — most of all — an example of what a person could achieve through the complete devotion of his every thought and moment to Hashem. To his *Chassidim,* the Rebbe reflected G-d's Holiness and *Malchus;* he was both man's advocate above and Hashem's below. The Rebbe also reached out to all *Yidden* — scholar and simple farmer alike — to help them see that they too were a special part of Hashem's Chosen People.

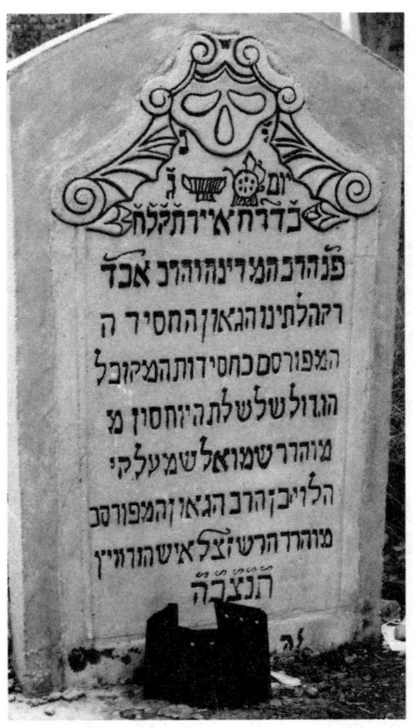

The Rebbe is a seventh-generation grandson, son after son, of Reb Shmuel Shmelke of Nikolsburg. The Rebbe visited his kever in (then) Czechoslovakia in 1985

Through the Rebbe's linking his *neshamah* to that of his *Chassid,* both were raised. The *Chassid* realized he could be much greater than he ever dreamed; and the Rebbe was elevated by the *chessed* of helping others. People from all over flocked to their Rebbe to ask him to help them, to bless them and make them worthy of blessings. They would enter his room one at a time, handing the Rebbe a *kvitel,* a small note containing their name, their mother's name and their request. The Rebbe would talk with them, bless them and save their notes to help remember their needs during his prayers.

Some Rebbes went even further. One Rabbi watched Reb Yaakov Yitzchak, the Chozeh of Lublin, receive several hundred such *kvitlach.* Later the Chozeh *davened* with his congregation, finishing at the same time as they did. The visiting Rabbi was surprised and asked the Chozeh how he could pray for so many different things for so many different people so quickly. "If you have true *ahavas Yisrael* it is quite simple," he said. "When someone tells me he is sick, I am sick with him; when a woman needs a child, I am childless with her; when someone is in trouble, I worry with him. When I *daven,* I only have to cry out: *Ribono Shel Olam,* help Yaakov Yitzchak ben Matel!"

The successes of this kind of "treatment" were soon told and retold, in hundreds of *myses* (stories) throughout Eastern Europe. Some Rebbes tried to downplay the miraculous; some even protested. They were afraid that the emphasis on physical miracles might overshadow the spiritual ones: the absolute faith of the *Chassid* in Hashem's *chessed* and in his Rebbe. The stories spread nonetheless. Since they were told mostly by the simple folk, rather than the scholars, they often have a beautiful childlike innocence about them. Still, you have to keep in mind that the Rebbes of the *myses* were, in real life, anything but simple. Reb Levi Yitzchak of Berditchev, for example, was not only a popular folk hero, he was also a great scholar and the author of the *Kedushas Levi,* a deep Chassidic commentary on the Torah.

As a little girl I was often sick with bronchitis, and I loved to hear my mother's *myses* as I lay in bed. My favorite stories involved Reb Meir Premishlaner, a famous *baal mofes* (miracle Rabbi), and the gentle Reb Zusia of Hanopoli. The unbounded love of Reb Zusia for everyone, despite all his suffering, was for me the greatest miracle of all. He stole my heart.

At the Rebbe's Court

The Jews in the *shtetlach* of Eastern Europe shared the same streets with their non-Jewish neighbors, but they had little in common with them. They had no sense of "belonging" to the governor or the king's royal officials, just as they had no sense of "belonging" to the parish priest and other local functionaries. For their part, local authorities treated the Jews as second-class citizens, or worse. The Rebbe, among his many other roles, met his *Chassidim's* need for participation in a larger brotherhood, for contact with greatness.

Coming to the Rebbe's court from their scattered communities, the *Chassidim* became part of a single great kingdom, with the Rebbe as their king. They were participants in a great happening, one affecting Heaven and Earth. This was especially true on the *Yom Tovim,* when thousands of *Chassidim* would assemble for a *tish* (gathering).

The Rebbe's majesty, not only in the lavish courts of Ruzhin and Sadigora, but even in the physically modest courts of Poland, inspired the *Chassidim* to incredible heights. When the Rebbe himself spoke to Chaim the water carrier, and truly concerned himself with his troubles, Chaim was no longer a water carrier. The Rebbe had spoken to him! He became a *Yisrael,* a "Prince of G-d," a son of

Avraham, Yitzchak and Yaakov, equal to anyone, and capable of great things in serving Hashem.

That was how the *Chassid* felt, but the Rebbe himself was usually the humblest of men. Reluctance to become a leader was almost a requirement for leadership. A *Misnagdishe* scholar once asked the Chozeh of Lublin, the leader of all the Chassidic Rebbes of Poland, why so many thousands of people flocked to see him. Wouldn't they do better to visit a *talmid chacham* like himself instead? The Chozeh told him, "You're right. I myself wonder why so many people come to see me; but maybe that is the answer. People come to see me, because I wonder why they do come. People don't come to see you, because you wonder why they don't come."

This great structure could not be transferred intact to America at the turn of the century; conditions were simply too different. Comparing the role of a Chassidic Rebbe in Europe to the way he was treated in America cannot help but make one sad. Yet, I don't want you to think that today's world has no relationship to this world of European *Chassidus*. Far from it! In the most important sense, only the externals have changed. On the inside, *Chassidus*, like the Torah itself, is part of every world.

Even if a little girl is all alone in Cleveland in the 1920s, if she can do a *chessed,* even when it is difficult for her and she doesn't want to, if she can overcome her *yetzer hara* and do it out of love for Hashem and out of love for a fellow Jew, such a little girl has also done something great and noble. She is serving the *Ribono Shel Olam* Himself. At least, that is what my mother always taught me. That is what I brought with me from Europe, and that is what my own personal *Chassidus* is all about.

On Yichus

Rebbes were not appointed by any outside authorities. Instead, the *Chassidim* themselves traveled from court to court until they found a Rebbe they could relate to, one who could understand them and help them serve Hashem. Some Rebbes drew *Chassidim* only from their own town and nearby districts. My grandfather, the Stryzover Zeide, was a Rebbe of this kind. Other Rebbes drew their followers from whole regions or countries. Still others, such as Rav Alter Ze'ev's (the Stryzover Zeide) great-grandfather, Rav Naftali Ropshitzer, drew *Chassidim* from all across Eastern Europe. It was not so much a difference in *tzidkus* or rank as a difference in function.

As time went on, however, *Chassidim* naturally tended to follow the Rebbe of their father, and the children of established *Rebbeim* tended to marry each other. This emphasis on marrying someone from a special *Rabbanishe* family (*yichus*), widespread among both *Chassidim* and *Misnagdim*, was based on two beliefs, both quite reasonable. Since children often — but not always — inherit physical features and gifts from their parents, it should be possible to inherit some of their special spiritual gifts as well. Also, one can assume that a child raised in the home of a *tzaddik* will benefit from the constant examples of *chessed* and *tzidkus* he sees all around him.

Although many people in Europe valued *yichus,* few understood its true worth better than the Stryzover Zeide's great-grandfather, Reb Naftali Ropshitzer, himself a great *meyuchas.* He used to say, "If a fellow without *yichus* is a great *tzaddik,* he gets up at midnight, learns until dawn, goes to the *mikveh,* then *davens* with *kavanah,* and works at Torah and *chessed* until lunchtime. When he sits down to his meal, he sighs and says, 'What is the real worth of all my Torah and *mitzvos*? How can I just sit down and eat like this?' But then he thinks, 'Well, considering where I come from and from where I started, maybe I haven't done too badly after all.' When a person with *yichus* does the same thing, he too sighs at lunch, but then he thinks, *'Gevalt!* Just look at who my fathers were and what they did. What would they think of me? How can I excuse myself to them or to G-d?' and his heart breaks inside him. Yes, *yichus* is a great thing, but you have to know how to use it."

My own *yichus* on my mother's side (see our family tree at the back of the book) begins with Reb Yaakov Reuven Linsker, a *talmid* of the Maggid of Mezritch, and a grandfather of Reb Naftali

Ropshitzer. It continued son after son down to my cousin, Reb Kalman Kalonimus. When he was killed in the *Churban* of Europe, this beautiful chain came to an end. Each link is a story of its own.

Reb Mendele Linsker

Reb Yaakov Linsker once attended an assembly of important rabbis in Katovitz, Poland. Between meetings to resolve halachic disputes, he met Reb Itzik'l Horowitz, the Rav of Hamburg. The two great rabbis began to discuss a potential match between their children. The Linsker Rav's son, Reb Mendele Linsker, was a brilliant young scholar; and the Hamburger Rav made it known that he was looking for just such a *talmid chacham* for his daughter, Baile. He promised the prospective *chassan* a big sack of gold *rendlach.*

After some preliminary discussions, the Linsker Rav, his wife and his son went to *shul* to have a quick glance at the prospective *kallah.* They found that the girl had a slight hunchback (perhaps because she was extremely studious and bent over her books for hours each day). Because of this handicap, the Linsker Rebbetzin was reluctant to agree to the *shidduch;* but Reb Mendele said that he would not shame the girl by canceling their meeting. He met her and was very impressed with her knowledge, her *midos* and her *yiras shamayim.* In short, Reb Mendele insisted on marrying her, despite her handicap, and his parents had to agree.

Shortly before the *chassanah,* Rav Itzik'l Hamburger called the *chassan* aside and told him that all the dowry money he had promised the newlyweds had been stolen, and that he had no way to support them. The young *chassan* said that he did not care about the money, and that his plans for the wedding remained unchanged.

After the wedding, during the week of *Sheva Brachos,* Rav Itzik'l Hamburger came in and gave the surprised *chassan* the "stolen" sack of gold coins. "I was only testing you," he explained. "I wanted to see if you were marrying my daughter for her money or for her *yiras shamayim.* Because you married her for her own sake,

Hashem will reward you with a son whose Torah will shine throughout the Jewish world." This *brachah* came true in their son, the Ropshitzer Rav.

The Ropshitzer Rav

Reb Naftali Tzvi Ropshitzer was quite famous, and there are many stories about him in the collections of Chassidic stories that are so popular these days. I particularly like the one about the pretentious young man who came to the Ropshitzer, all dressed in white, to tell him about his dream.

"I had a dream," he said, "that I am destined to be a Rebbe. Do you think that I should declare myself as a Rebbe to the world?" The Ropshitzer simply said, "No." Not easily discouraged, the man came back a few days later to the Ropshitzer, with the same dream and the same question. This time the Rebbe told him, "If you dream that you're a Rebbe, *maynt es gornisht,* that doesn't mean anything. Your *Chassidim* have to dream that you're a Rebbe!"

The Ropshitzer was a great scholar, and he wrote a well-known sefer, *Zera Kodesh.* He was best known, however, for his incredible wit. He even acted as *badchan* at many a *chassanah,* because the Talmud praises the *badchanim* who can make people laugh and forget their troubles. People didn't realize that the Ropshitzer used his constant joking to hide the miraculous things he did in heaven and on earth. Only on his deathbed did he call in his *Chassidim* and tell them, "I want you to know that I never told a joke in my life."

The Ropshitzer was actually my *zeide's* great-grandfather, but I didn't feel the distance so much. In fact, he has always been one of my favorite *zeides,* because he always wanted to make others happy.

The Melitzer Rav

The eldest son of the Ropshitzer Rav was Reb Yankele Melitzer, who inherited a famous miracle-working cane from his father. My mother used to tell me marvelous stories about that cane.

Reb Yankele Melitzer had a *Chassid* who earned his living as an innkeeper. One day the old *poritz,* his landlord, died; and the *poritz's* son, a vicious anti-Semite, refused to continue renting him the inn. The *Chassid,* who had no other means of support, came to Reb Yankele and begged him for advice on how to persuade the Jew-hater to renew his lease.

"Don't worry," the Rebbe said, as he walked over to the window, pointed his cane and — "Boom!" — made a sound like a gun. Then he walked back to his seat, sat down and told the *Chassid* to go back home. All would now be well. The puzzled *Chassid* looked at his watch to keep himself from laughing at the strange goings-on. Finally, he rode home, somehow reassured by his visit to the Rebbe, but still wondering how he was going to handle the new *poritz.* Before he reached the little bridge that led to his town, his son came running out to meet him.

"Tatti, Tatti," his son called out. "The new *poritz* went out hunting today and was shot dead by a stray bullet!" The *Chassid* could not believe his ears. It was a real miracle. He asked his son when the *poritz* had been killed. The "accident" had happened at three o'clock, exactly the same moment when the Melitzer Rebbe had pretended to shoot with his wonder-working cane.

Another time, one of the Melitzer's daughters was missing, lost in the forest around the city of Melitz. Miraculously, the Melitzer Rav sensed her problem and sent a messenger to her, together with his famous cane, to help her find her way home. When she returned safe and sound, he told her, "I sent you a good guide to show you the way out of the forest!"

The Sendyszover Rav

Reb Avraham Horowitz, the Sendyszover Rav and my great-grandfather, was the son of the Melitzer Rav. I don't know much about his first Rebbetzin, but his second Rebbetzin was named Raichel, and I am named after her. She was a daughter of Rav Shmuel Hacohen Katz. Reb Shmuel, in turn, was the son-in-law of the Pshevarsker Rav, author of *Meshiv K'halachah,* and a grandson of Reb Shmuel Shmelke of Nikolsburg (through his daughter).

The Stryzover Zeide

My *zeide,* Reb Alter Ze'ev, was the son of the Sendyszover Rav. He was not only my personal *zeide,* but almost everyone called him "the Stryzover Zeide," a way of showing their closeness and love. Since I have told you some *myses* about my other relatives, I will tell you some about the Stryzover Zeide and Bobeh Yehudis as well.

Saved on Sukkos

During the fall holiday of Sukkos, Jews live outside in special booths, called *sukkos,* which remind us of Hashem's help and protection after we left Egypt and wandered for 40 years in the desert. The *sukkah* is thus a symbol of how Hashem protects the Jewish people at all times. Rav Alter Ze'ev's *sukkah* was built on the third-floor porch of his house, and he lived there the entire Sukkos. Our family decorated the *sukkah* with colorful fruits and pictures, and Zeide would sit there and learn Torah for hours at a time.

In 1914 World War I began, causing great suffering to the Jews of Eastern Europe. One year the Russian and Austrian armies were fighting in our area. The Russians had decided that the Jews were all spies and enemies, perhaps because they spoke Yiddish which sounded like German to them. They had already arrested the *Rosh Hakahal* (President of the Jewish Community) and the mayor of Stryzov as "prisoners of war." Then they headed towards our house to capture Reb Alter Ze'ev as well.

Someone saw them coming down the street and ran to warn Bobeh Yehudis. She quickly climbed the stairs to the *sukkah* and told Zeide to hide. He flatly refused to budge, saying: "*Vee hab ich a besseren bahelternish vi bei dem Ribono Shel Olam in der sukkah!* Where would I have a better hiding place than by the *Ribono Shel Olam* in the *sukkah*!" So he calmly continued learning.

Finally the Russian troops arrived and burst into the house. Grandfather still sat quietly learning. They charged up the first two flights of stairs and locked the *Rosh Hakahal* and the mayor in a room on the second floor. Then they started climbing up the third flight of stairs to seize the "Rabbiner." Just then someone blew a loud whistle and yelled, "The Austrian army is coming! Run for your lives!" The Russian soldiers began shouting at each other and running in all directions. Soon the house was empty of soldiers, and the "prisoners" on the second floor were released. Secure in his faith, Zeide remained quietly learning in his big green *sukkah*, undisturbed.

The Garden Woman

Bobeh Yehudis had a very devoted peasant woman who worked for her. Every day she came to work in our vegetable garden, to fetch our water and to do much of the heavy housework. This woman loved my grandmother very much.

Once the peasant woman's little hut caught fire and burned down. She was left penniless. She ran to the local priest to ask for help, but he only gave her a few *groschen*. Then she came crying to my grandmother, who asked her how much money she needed to rent two rooms, until she could somehow resettle. Bobeh Yehudis gave her the money and then went to her closet and took out some clothes for the woman's children. Finally, she added some more money for food.

Her arms loaded with clothing, the peasant woman began crying. "Why are you crying?" my grandmother asked. "Isn't it enough money?" "Yes, yes," she said, "it's enough. I'm crying because, when I went to my own people, they did nothing to help me. You are Jewish, and yet you are doing everything to help me."

Towards the end of World War I, food was rationed in Poland. The local priest administered the food distribution for Stryzov, saying who should get more and who should get less. Naturally, there were intense arguments about the food distribution among the people. This same peasant woman, who was used to the *kedushah* of our home, used to call out to the priest: "What are you doing here, busying yourself with food stamps and politics? You should be sitting and learning like the Rabbi of the town. He learns and prays. What are you doing here?"

The First Pogrom

In 1898, when my mother was four years old, this same peasant woman came to Bobeh Yehudis and warned her about a pogrom. The family quickly made plans to escape. Reb Alter Ze'ev boarded a coach with his *gabbai;* Bobeh Yehudis boarded another coach with her two married daughters and a baby; and a neighbor boarded a third coach together with her child, my mother and the baby of one of my aunts. All three coaches were supposed to rush to the train station. If they got separated, they were all to meet at the home of our relatives in Zeshov (Reicha), a short train ride away.

Only my mother's coach, the one headed by our neighbor, actually reached the train station. The other coaches vanished! Worse, the frightened neighbor had no money to pay for the train tickets. She rushed to the bank in the train station to try to withdraw money from my grandmother's account, but the clerk refused, saying that he could not give her any money without my grandmother's signature.

All around the town, sounds could be heard of Jews being beaten by the mobs and screaming. In despair, the neighbor and the children rushed back to the train platform. Suddenly, a little old Jew with an old-fashioned moneybag mysteriously appeared. He walked across the tracks, came over to the children and asked them why they were crying. "We need to take the train, but we have no money for the ticket," they cried. The stranger took out his moneybag and counted out the coins they needed, and they all boarded the train to Zeshov. On the train, Mother was crying. The little old man patted her head and said, "Don't cry, little girl. Everything will be all right. Soon you will be with your father and mother."

Finally, the neighbor, the children and the old man arrived at my cousins' house in Zeshov. After our relatives had heard the whole story, they looked around for the kind old man. They wanted to thank him and to pay him for the tickets; but he had already disappeared. Our neighbor always referred to him as *Eliyahu HaNavi.*

What happened meanwhile to my grandparents? Neither ever reached the train station. The mob attacked their coaches before they could escape. Reb Alter Ze'ev ran into a barn owned by the town's non-Jewish doctor; but the angry mob set the barn afire. The doctor's daughter saw him from the window; but she knew that the Rav would not enter the house with her there alone, not even to save his life. So she secretly threw him the house keys and left. Zeide then quietly let himself into the house and was saved. Bobeh Yehudis and her two older daughters, with the baby, ran into a nearby Jewish house. They barricaded the door with the heavy tin water barrel, and they too were saved.

The Second Pogrom

The same peasant woman warned our family about another pogrom, just after I was born. I was born on the second of Nissan, and the *goyim* started their rampage 12 days later, on *Erev Pesach.* The drunken mob surrounded our house, and announced that the first Jews they were going to kill were the "Rabbiner" and his family. Our peasant woman darkened the whole house, so it looked like we were not at home. We all hid in the attic, and Mother nursed me the whole time, so I would not cry out and give us away.

We had a big double front door. The maid, a broad husky woman, stood with her arms crossed and refused to let the mob cross the threshold. "Over my dead body," she said. "I'm the housekeeper here, and if anything here is missing, I'll be liable for it. Don't you dare come in here, or I'll beat you up!" Then she slammed the doors and locked them tight.

That slowed the mob down; but they were soon singing and drinking again, getting ready to break down the door. Suddenly the sky turned dark and a huge hailstorm crashed down, scattering the mob in all directions! It was a true miracle.

Once the streets were clear, our loyal peasant woman came up to the attic and told us that we could all come down. She lit the kerosene lamps (it was already *Yom Tov*), lit the fire so the women could *bentch licht*, and Reb Alter Ze'ev and the family sat down to the *Pesach seder*, my first in this world.

My Father's Family

My father's *yichus* also goes back to the Ropshitzer Rav, through his son Reb Eliezer (Lazer'l), the Dzikover Rav. His granddaughter Chana married the Zhabner Rav, Rav Yaakov Yitzchak Ungar, my great-grandfather.

Rav Lazer'l's "Sefer"

Once Reb Lazer'l dreamed that he and the Rebbe Reb Melech of Lizhensk were in a room lined with shelves of beautiful *sefarim*. The Rebbe Reb Melech took one of the *sefarim* and said, "I am giving you this *sefer* as a gift." When Reb Lazer'l told this dream to his father, the Ropshitzer Rav said, "You must have done something very special to merit this; You will have a son who will write a great *sefer.*" Reb Lazer'l explained that he had helped two poor sons of the Rebbe Reb Melech who had just visited their town; but that it had been purely *l'shem Shamayim,* without expecting a reward.

Rav Lazer'l had discovered that the sons did not have warm coats for the winter. He immediately gave away one of his two fur-lined coats to the younger brother, and ordered a new fur-lined coat from a tailor for the older brother. Then, he quietly helped them collect some money, so they could go back home and support their families.

It is said that the Rebbe Reb Melech, before he was *niftar,* had prayed that his children would remain poor but religious. Then he added that he would intervene in Heaven for anyone who helped them or their children for seven generations. In time, Reb Lazer'l's dream came true. His son, Reb Meir (Meir'l) Dzikover, wrote a famous Chassidic *sefer*, the *Imre Noam.*

Reb Meir'l Dzikover

Rav Meir'l played the lottery only once in his life — and won! He used the prize money to build a new *yeshivah.* My father's father, Reb Yehudah Ungar, the Sokolover Rav and the son of Reb Meir'l's oldest daughter, Chana, studied there. Reb Meir'l used to walk up and down the rows of tables in the *yeshivah* dining room, reciting *divrei Torah* while the *bachurim* were still eating their meals.

When Reb Meir'l's younger daughter, Hinde, married Reb Yisrael, later the Vizhnitzer Rebbe, Bobeh Chana prepared an elaborate wedding feast, with numerous roasted chickens and many side dishes. Reb Meir'l was displeased that she served chicken. He told her, "Instead of killing so many *nefashos* to serve chicken, you could have killed just a few *behamos* and served beef!"

At that time, the typical living quarters for a newlywed couple was an *alker mit a kich,* a bedroom with a tiny kitchenette. The typical main dish was *jemnekis* (potatoes) and more *jemnekis.* Thanks to Reb Meir'l's generosity, the future Vizhnitzer Rebbe and his

Rebbetzin had their own apartment and could have afforded to dine on roast beef, even on weekdays. Despite all the luxuries waiting for him at home, Reb Yisrael ate a simple lunch in the *yeshivah* with all the other *bachurim*. Reb Meir'l once asked him, "Why do you sit here eating bread when, at home, you could be eating roast beef!" The young man answered, "I would rather have bread and water while I listen to you teach Torah and *Chassidus* than eat the best roast in the world!"

The new couple also attended the lavish family breakfasts of rolls, butter, herring and hard spiced cheeses that Reb Meir'l prepared for all his children, grandchildren and the *bachurim* living with them. Reb Meir'l used to start the meal by saying: *"Ir zeyt alles. Ir muzt nisht alles haben. Ir muzt nish alles essen* — You can look at everything, but you can not have everything; and you can not eat everything." It was Reb Meir'l's lesson in how to approach all the luxuries of this world. Enjoy, but only in moderation, only with self-control.

Rav Yehudah Ungar

My grandfather, Rav Yehudah Ungar, was the grandson of Reb Meir'l. He was a great *talmid chacham,* who wrote commentaries on his grandfather's book, the *Imre Noam.* He was first a Rav in Sokolov; but he could not stand all the local squabbles. Eventually he gave up his position and moved to Rzcszow, and then to Novytark, a small town near Zakipane. He lived to the ripe old age of 93, dying in 1939, only three months before the Nazis invaded Poland.

The Sokolover Rav's Rebbetzin, Bobeh Leah, was the daughter of another great *talmid chacham,* Rav Yeshayah (Shiyele) Charif. The Charif family is a famous one, with 17 generations of Rabbinic *yichus,* dating all the way back to the *Geonim.* Rav Shiyele Charif was a well-known scholar, and a grandnephew of the Rama. I once met a man who had known Reb Shiyele, and he told me that the Rav's face was as radiant as an angel's. After Reb Shiyele's passing, his children could not decipher the volumes of *chiddushim* (new Torah thoughts) he had written. After questioning the maid, they realized that, in his excitement, he had often continued writing from his sheet of paper right onto the tablecloth! The maid had dutifully washed the tablecloth regularly and, with it, many fragments of his *chiddushim.*

Even after my parents' divorce, my mother and her father-in-law, the Sokolover Rav, remained on good terms. He would even quote her *divrei Torah*! This quite amazed my brother-in-law, Reb Menashe Frankel, who once went to Novytark for Shabbos and heard these *divrei Torah* for himself. My mother's level of scholarship was uncommon among the European Jewish women of her time.

Mother herself took the divorce calmly, believing in the Talmud's promise that "*Kal mah d'aveid Rachmana l'tav aveid* — Whatever Hashem does is for the best." She later felt that her divorce, which seemed so difficult at first, was Hashem's way of bringing us to America and saving us from the Churban in Europe. In that way, I became the sole survivor of my father's long line of *Rabbanim.* With Hashem's help, I, and my own dear family, were able to carry on their task and to help pass it on to the next generation.

THREE

To America

Aunt Brucha

Aunt Brucha was six years older than my mother. She was married in Poland to Rav Yehoshua Heshel Eichenstein, who later became the Zydachover Rebbe of Chicago. They decided to emigrate to America in the early 1920s, although my grandparents were very much against it. In those days, going to America was frowned upon, since there were few strictly religious communities or facilities, and it was very difficult to be an observant Jew there. Indeed, many of the new immigrants quickly became "American" and left their European religious roots far behind. In Europe, leaving for America seemed almost like leaving *Yiddishkeit*. Aunt Brucha left anyway and, despite all odds, raised a family of outstanding Rabbanim and *talmidei chachamim*. Her husband predicted, "There will come a time when people will want to come to America; and they won't be able to" — a prediction that proved all too true.

As was usual in those days, Uncle Yehoshua Heshel went to America first, to pave the way, while Aunt Brucha stayed in Chodorov. Once in America, Rav Eichenstein, who lived in Chicago, met Rav Meir Leifer, the Nadvorna Rebbe of Clevelander. He was very impressed and they became close friends. Rav Eichenstein wrote my mother suggesting a *shidduch* with Rav Leifer, who had also been divorced. When she agreed, Rav Leifer traveled all the way to Poland to meet her. He was particularly glad to hear that my mother had already had two children, since he was childless.

Rav Yissachar Ber Leifer

Rav Leifer's father, Rav Yissachar Ber (Bertze), the Nadvorna Rebbe of Satmar, was a great *tzaddik*. When his *shamash* came to America, he told me that he had once knocked on a door in Budapest and asked if he and Reb Bertze could have a room for the night. The lady of the house said no. When the *shamash* told Reb Bertze this, he ordered his *shamash* to knock on the door again and to tell the lady of the house that he was the six-year-old red-haired boy who had once given her a *brachah*. When she heard this, she ran out, welcomed Reb Bertze warmly and treated him with special care.

She later told the *shamash* that she had gone to Reb Bertze's father, Rav Mordechai of Nadvorna, for a *brachah*, because she was childless. There were many other people there and, although she waited day after day for a whole week, she was unable to get in to see the Rebbe. Since she had to be home for Shabbos, she had no choice but to leave without a *brachah;* and she began to cry. A little red-haired boy came by and asked her why she was crying. She explained that she desperately wanted a *brachah* to have children, and it was now too late for her to see the Rebbe. The little boy (Reb Bertze) told her, "Don't cry, I will give you a *brachah*." He did; and the lady eventually had seven or eight children!

Reb Bertze had a special way of looking at things. Whenever he saw an old man, he used to say, "He has more *mitzvos* than I have." Whenever he saw a young man, he used to say, "He has less *aveiros* (sins) than I have." When he held a *tish*, he would not let anyone stand in back of his chair, because he said that angels stood in back of him. A *meshulach* once told us how Reb Bertze had cured his sister, who had suffered a nervous breakdown. Reb Bertze told her to come to his *shul* Friday night to hear him say *Kabbalas Shabbos*. She did so and, soon after, she became well.

Rav Meir Leifer

Rav Meir Leifer, the Nadvorna-Clevelander Rebbe, his younger sister and his two older brothers were orphaned when he was only a year and a half old. Their father's second wife was young and inexperienced in taking care of small children and, in fact, they were somewhat neglected.

My stepfather, Rav Meir Leifer, the Nadvorna-Clevelander Rebbe, was a tremendous baal chessed

Just around this time, an old woman a neighbor, became very ill. The family called the *Chevra Kaddisha*, lit candles and said *Tehillim*. Suddenly, the old woman sat up in bed and said, "Everybody can go home now. I'm well!" She explained that Rav Leifer's mother had appeared to her in a dream and said, "If you promise to bathe, feed and take care of my children, I promise that you will have a *refuah shleimah*."

"I agreed," she said, "and the Rebbetzin put her left hand under my pillow and brought out a small bottle. She gave me three teaspoons of medicine, and then I woke up feeling perfectly fine." The woman kept her promise and took care of the Rebbetzin's young children. Later, when Rav Leifer became a Rebbe, she became a follower of his.

The First Marriage

When Rav Leifer grew up, he married a fine young woman and became a Rebbe in Budapest. He did not believe that *naddan* money had *brachah,* so he spent most of it on furniture so they could live comfortably and help guests. He and his Rebbetzin made a point of helping the many Jewish refugees who came to Budapest during World War I.

Unfortunately, they remained childless and since Rav Leifer very much wanted children, they eventually divorced, by mutual consent. Rav Leifer still cared for his former wife, and he gave her all of their furnishings and silver and the equivalent of several thousand dollars in cash. About all he kept for himself was his clothing, *sefarim, tefillin* and a Chanukah *menorah* that had been made from Reb Bertze's melted-down spoons.

Rav Leifer moved to America shortly after his divorce, and he settled in Cleveland, Ohio, where he was known as the Nadvorna Rebbe. Later, when we moved to Williamsburg (1933), he was known as the Clevelander Rebbe. In both places, he led *Chassidim,* accepted *kvitlach,* held a Shabbos *tish* and gave out *brachos.* He always said, "People need a *brachah,* and Hashem has *rachmanus.* The *brachos* come true because Hashem wants to help people, not because of me."

Rav Leifer's first Rebbetzin married another European Rebbe; but she never had children. Years later, when my sister Chaya Yehudis was born, she wrote a letter to Rav Leifer offering her congratulations. "Although we are not supposed to communicate," she wrote, "I just wanted to say that I am delighted to hear that Hashem has granted you a child." In fact, her sister remained in contact with us for some time after we came to America.

Mother Remarries

I was only about five years old when Rav Leifer traveled to Europe to meet my mother. I knew nothing about his visit, or even about their marriage a few weeks later. Instead, I remember that I was sleeping later than usual in Aunt Brucha's house in Chodorov, when my cousins woke me up and told me the shocking news: Mother had remarried! This was very confusing to me at the time.

When I finally met my stepfather, I liked him right away. He was a pleasant man who loved children, and he was a true *tzaddik*. Eventually, I became very close with his family, and his nieces and nephews in New York are still like cousins to me.

Leah Stays Behind

So we were going to America! At least Mother and I, but not my sister Leah. When we lived in Stryzov, Mother often volunteered to go out of town to help her married sisters when they had babies; Leah became very close to Bobeh Yehudis. Since my grandparents could not bear to see Leah leave, she stayed behind in Stryzov. My grandparents were also afraid that she would not be able to live a fully religious life in America.

Although we were separated by a wide ocean, Leah and I always remained very close. Years later, before she was lost in the Churban, Leah told me that Rav Leifer had promised her the sun, the moon and the stars, plus a new bedroom set, if she would come with us to America.

Passports

Getting passports in those days was no simple matter. My mother, who was now married to a "Hungarian," left for Budapest with my stepfather to get Hungarian citizenship and a Hungarian passport. Meanwhile, Uncle Chaim Yehudah took me to the government office in Stryzov to apply for my Polish passport. It was quite an experience just to have my photograph taken! I still have and treasure that old photograph.

My passport photograph, taken in Stryzov, Poland, when I was six years old

Uncle Chaim Yehudah went into the mayor's office to speak to the mayor and left me outside in the waiting room. I was surrounded by tall Polish peasants, who were also sitting and waiting for their turn. They looked like giants to me, and I was terribly afraid of them.

I waited and waited for my uncle to come out of the inner office; it seemed to me that he was there for hours. Perhaps he was not really gone for all that long, but it seemed that way to me at the time. For a little girl, time can pass very slowly (when you grow up, it passes all too quickly). Anyway, I became impatient and decided to go home by myself. I must have been a pretty independent six-year-old, because it was a cold wintry day and quite a long walk. Since I had no one to hold onto, I soon tripped on a steep hill of snow and fell fast asleep. Luckily, some passerby recognized me, woke me up and walked me to our doorstep.

I remember that I came inside and went straight in to the nursery, where I used to sleep. I went right to bed with my coat still on! "I'm just tired, Bobeh, it's nothing serious," I said, as Bobeh Yehudis came in with worried questions. She immediately saw that I was burning with a high fever and called the doctor, who said that I had come down with another bout of chronic bronchitis or possibly pneumonia.

You don't know how lucky you are to have modern medicine. They didn't use antibiotics for pneumonia in those days. Instead, the doctors tried to help me with *bahnkes* (sucking cups). Small hot glass cups were put on my back. As these cooled, the vacuum drew the skin into small mounds. The doctors cut these to let out "excess" blood, which was supposed to reduce the fever. The cups added a bit of warmth; but the process left my poor little back covered with bloody painful welts.

The Voyage

Finally I recovered. Then Mother and Rav Leifer returned and we set off for America together. First we traveled by train through Germany. When we reached Cherbourg in France, we boarded a beautiful ocean-liner, *The Paris.* (*The Paris* was later sunk by the Nazis in World War II.) Since Rav Leifer had a close friend in the shipping company, we were given first-class cabins. During the journey, Rav Leifer played chess with the French captain; but he made sure to let him win a few times, just to stay on his good side. The ship always docked on Shabbos, so we were unable to go ashore until we reached America.

I really got to know my stepfather — I called him *"Fetter"* (Uncle) — on the ship; and I developed a great love for him. He was always attentive and had lots of patience. In retrospect, I see now that he was also wise and understanding. He realized my conflicting feelings about my mother's remarriage, and he took them in stride. One day, in our cabin, I told Mother that she should take my father back as her husband. "And what will happen to Fetter?" she asked. "Don't worry," I said, "*I* will marry him!"

The Doll

Rav Leifer had bought a special oversized doll in a carriage as a gift for the daughter of the president of his Cleveland *shul.* On the boat, he let me use the doll; and I loved sitting her up in her carriage and playing with her. Once — it was wintertime, just before Chanukah — the stormy sea made the boat roll suddenly. Before I could do anything about it, the carriage fell over and the doll broke its nose. It wasn't my fault, but I felt very bad for the doll. There it was, all of a sudden, with a broken nose! Then I remembered how Reb Alter Ze'ev never let us have a doll with a full face. He would always cut off the nose, explaining to us that a Jew should never have a statue or an idol.

Soon afterwards, I had a nightmare. I dreamt that one of my cousins had bitten a hole in the back of my hand! The dream was so real that I remember it to this day. This cousin really used to bite me whenever I didn't do exactly what she wanted. My aunt used to say, "Bite her back!" but I couldn't do it. I had too much *rachmonus.*

Miracle at Ellis Island

As soon as we reached Ellis Island, Rav Leifer was arrested! Someone who opposed his *Rabbanus* in Cleveland had written outrageous lies to the American authorities. They said that Rav Leifer had abandoned his wife and 10 children in Europe, and was running off with some *shiksa* to America. This "*shiksa*" was supposed to be my mother! This was the most ridiculous accusation imaginable. My mother was such a *tzadekes* that she didn't even wear a wig, only a full cloth hair-covering.

We spent a terrible night in custody on Ellis Island. We were put in bunkbeds in a room with a wide open window that did not close. All night long, the wind blew fiercely. Mother spent the whole night holding her black Persian-lamb coat over the window to block the wind. I had just recovered from pneumonia in Poland, and she was afraid that I might have a relapse.

The next day we had to appear before an American judge. By a miracle, the court interpreter for the case was a Jew from Stryzov, our hometown! Of course he knew my grandfather, the Stryzover Zeide, and his whole *yichus.* He immediately told the judge how ridiculous the accusation was — how could the Stryzover Zeide's daughter be a *shiksa!* — and the judge threw the case out of court.

As you can see, "Hashem sends the *refuah* (cure) before the *makah* (illness)." Otherwise, how could an American court interpreter from Stryzov, Poland just happen to appear at just that time, at just that spot!

FOUR

Cleveland

A New World

Once we arrived in America, we boarded a train and traveled straight to Cleveland. There we lived in a large house, a former mansion, in Skoville. The building was divided into a *shul,* Rabbi Leifer's office, the kitchen, and then separate bedrooms, living rooms and guest rooms. Altogether, there were 24 rooms and each door had a number; mine was number 8. In Stryzov my grandparents also had a big house; and I was used to sharing the communal space with all my aunts, uncles and cousins, who each lived in their own apartments. But in Cleveland, for the first time, we had constant guests who were not members of our family.

Culture shock was a far more serious problem. Compared to Europe, America was, in those days, a Jewish wasteland. Most of the few Jewish facilities that existed were concentrated in New York City. Cleveland was a *galus* (exile) within a *galus.*

I have already mentioned the grandeur of the Rebbe's position in Europe. In America it was just the opposite. The new immigrants were often the most "enlightened," materialistic and least religious part of the American Jewish community. Freed from the peer pressures of their communities, and subjected to the economic and social pressures of America, the immigrants "optional" religious observance dropped to incredible depths. Often even the most basic *mitzvos* — *Shabbos, tefillin, kashrus* — were simply abandoned, leaving only a taste of Jewishness behind. To them a Rebbe, far from being a *melech* (king), was an embarrassment, the symbol of everything "old fashioned" they wanted to leave behind. At best, he was tolerated as "just another Rabbi."

In those days, the religious community itself was scattered and disorganized. The few Jews who remained *Chassidim* all held by different *Rebbeim* who, in any case, were 5,000 miles away. What the Rebbe's father, Pinchas Dovid Horowitz, accomplished in the 1920s and '30s in Boston was to unite these uprooted *Yidden* into a *Chassidus* all their own, an American *Chassidus*.

Rav Leifer faced many of these same problems in Cleveland. I remember my best friend in Skoville, a little girl who lived next door. Every time I came over, her parents would play records with funny songs about Rebbes, like *"Oy, oy, der Rebbe geit."* This supposed joke was repeated time after time and, of course, I felt hurt that they were making fun of the Nadvorna Rebbe, my stepfather. Adjusting wasn't easy.

In an American School

School was a particularly touchy problem. In the early 1920s, there were no Bais Yaakov schools for girls (I went to the first Bais Yaakov school in New York in 1936). Still, the law said that I must go to school or my parents could be arrested. So six-year-old Raichel bas Rochma Miril from Stryzov, Poland found herself in a Cleveland public school the first autumn after we arrived in America.

The day began without problems. I already knew some English by then; and I was very proud when the teacher wrote down my English name: Raichel Horowitz (I used my mother's maiden name). Still, I was not used to going to school with non-Jews. During recess, in the schoolyard, the other children asked me who I was and where I was from. I told them that I was from Poland and that I was Jewish. They said, "You're Jewish? Oh, you killed our god." I said, "What? Who? I never even heard of him." This made them even more angry. They began to yell and scream at me, calling me names. I came home very upset, and very emotional.

More Illness

It didn't help matters that I was often sick with chronic respiratory illnesses and allergies. One day, I must have been about seven, I came home from school during a big downpour. Mother wasn't home; and I was afraid to stay indoors. The elderly *shochet* who lived with us used to try to catch my ankle with his cane and trip me up, so I stayed outside in the rain until Mother came home.

I was thoroughly chilled and caught pneumonia again. I became so ill that I passed out. When I regained consciousness, I could hear people around me talking; but I couldn't answer them. Mother tried to speak to me and I wanted to answer her, to tell her my name and so on, but I could not. Because the local doctors had already given up on me, Mother eventually sent for five out-of-town specialists. One was a prominent pediatrician from St. Louis. After examining me, he promised her that I would get well.

Mother wanted to give me an additional name, a common *segulah* to help people who are very ill; but Rav Leifer told her that his family's custom was not to change or add names, because that would take the person away from his *shoresh* (source). "She will live out her years with the name she has," he told her.

When I began to feel better, Mother hired nurses to take care of me around the clock. I remember watching one nurse powdering her nose with a compact, and I was fascinated by that. My first words upon returning to consciousness were, "I need a compact to powder my nose!" A woman friend, who was staying in the hospital with my mother, ran straight to the drugstore and bought me a compact. Like most seven-year-olds I wanted to act "grownup"; and I was thrilled to be able to powder my nose just like the nurse. Mother was even more thrilled that I was well again.

Rav Leifer's Midos

My stepfather, the Clevelander Rebbe, was a real *tzaddik.* He was so honest that I still find it difficult to tell even a "white lie" for the sake of diplomacy and peace. My mother, however, used to tell me: *"A ligen tor men nisht zogen; ober dem emes, muz men nisht zogen* — You shouldn't tell a lie, but you don't *have* to tell the truth (if it will hurt someone)." They both taught me about the importance of *hachnasas orchim* and lending a helping hand whenever possible. Mother always had a house full of guests, because Rav Leifer did not enjoy eating a meal unless he could share it with someone.

More than Skin Deep

Rav Leifer gave marvelous *brachos* and advice to people. Once, during the Depression Years, a young woman with a severe case of eczema on her face and hands came in to see him. Because of her skin condition, nobody would go out with her and she could not find a job. She was terribly unhappy. Rav Leifer promised her that Hashem would help her. He told her not to wash her hands and face with soap and water at all, but rather to use rice powder. "With time," he said, "the eczema will disappear." Later, Mother, who had also talked with the young woman, asked him how he could have raised her hopes so high. Wasn't that cruel, since her skin condition seemed so severe and incurable?

Less than a year later, the young woman returned to our home to ask for another *brachah.* Mother simply did not recognize her. Her face and hands were perfectly clear, and she had a big smile! There was a young man with her, whom she introduced as her *chassan.* She told us that she had also found a job.

After she had left, Mother said to Rav Leifer: "If I hadn't seen this with my own eyes, I wouldn't have believed it. You must be a tremendous *tzaddik* if you can do something like that!" Rav Leifer told her, "I didn't do it. She had perfect faith that Hashem would accept my prayer, and Hashem had *rachmanus* on her. I certainly can't take the credit for that."

Loneliness

Still, things were very hard for me in Cleveland. I was young and quite different from all my schoolmates and, most of the time, I was very lonely. My sister Leah was in Stryzov, playing with all our cousins, and surrounded by our grandparents, uncles and aunts. In Cleveland I was surrounded by *goyim* and not-so-religious Jewish neighbors. It was also hard to adjust to suddenly being an "only child." I would beg my mother to tell me stories about the family I missed so much. That is how I know so many stories about our family in Europe.

Sunday was the hardest day. All my neighborhood friends spent their Sundays at the movies, and I couldn't find anyone to play with me. My parents would not let me go to the movies (a decision I can certainly understand today), so I just stayed home and helped Mother clean up after Shabbos.

Housework

When Mother arrived in America, she was not used to washing dishes or cooking, because we had always had plenty of household help in Stryzov. Her hands were lily white. Now she had to learn how to cook, to bake and to wash dishes.

Whenever she had a spare moment, however, she would look into a *sefer* and learn.

A housewife worked much harder in those days. Very few strictly kosher products were available. We used to have *cholov Yisrael* milk delivered to our house; but it was unpasteurized, so we had to boil it before we could use it. Then Mother would make her own butter and cheese. We also had to make our own *challos, lokshen* (noodles) and *farfel.* I still remember how, on *lokshen*-making day, there was noodle dough stretched thin on tablecloths spread over every available surface. Wherever you turned, you saw *lokshen* dough.

We were fortunate to have an excellent kosher *shomer Shabbos* bakery nearby, Ungar's Bakery, which is still there to this day. They baked delicious bread and they made a wonderful pound cake, covered with chocolate and coconut bars. This was a tremendous treat for me, because I could not buy kosher candy or ice cream anywhere. This was the only special treat I could have.

The Katchkele Club

Still, all was not bleak in Cleveland. Rav Leifer was a real Chassidic Rebbe and conducted a beautiful Friday night *tish,* with lots of singing, *divrei Torah* and *Rebbeishe myses.* When I was a little girl, I used to sit on a big leather armchair in the dining room and fall asleep listening to the Clevelander *Chassidim* singing Shabbos *niggunim.*

On *Motzaei Shabbos* Rav Leifer held a *Melaveh Malkah,* which everyone called "The Katchkele Club." It was named after the two roast ducks (*katchkelech*) that were served each week. It was so much fun that I almost didn't mind not going to the movies on Sundays. The Katchkele Club was far more fun than any movie.

The ducks were brought by two Clevelander *Chassidim* who were also *shochtim.* One of them, who had a face like a *malach,* was the *melamed* who taught me how to *daven* when I was eight years old. Another of the Clevelander's "*Chassidim*" was actually a *Misnagid,* who used to come to the *Melaveh Malkah* with seven whole herrings. I used to strip them and cut them up into slices, the way people do with matjes herring. Since he was a *Litvak* and, as is well known, *Litvaks* eat a lot of herring, this man used to tell Rav Leifer every time he brought his herrings, "A *Litvak* can't go for long without his *landsleit* (fellow countrymen)!"

Finally, when everything was ready, about two dozen *Chassidim* would come, make a *motzi,* taste the herring and the roast duck, and sit up late into the night listening to Rav Leifer's stories in Yiddish about the great *tzaddikim.* I used to stay up late too, listening to them, and that is another reason I know so many tales.

An Expensive Song

Once a certain *meshulach* came to stay for Shabbos; and he told this story about the special *niggun* he taught The Katchkele Club.

There was a young man who was a big *talmid chacham,* but also a big *batlan* (ne'er-do-well). One day his father-in-law got tired of giving him free room and board. Instead, he gave him 10,000 *guilden* and told him, "Here's a horse and buggy. Go out and become a merchant! Tomorrow is the market day in the big town. Buy some merchandise there, and earn your living by selling it in the smaller towns!"

The young man took the money and rode along to the marketplace the following morning. Along the way, he heard a shepherd singing a beautiful song. "How much money would it cost for you to teach me that lovely song?" asked the young would-be merchant. The shepherd hemmed and hawed, and the two of them bickered for most of the morning, until finally the shepherd said, "I'll teach you my song, but only if you pay me 10,000 *guilden*!" The price was absurd, but the young man had become enthralled by the glorious tune, and finally he decided to give up his entire fortune to the shepherd in exchange for the song.

When he returned home, his father-in-law asked him straightaway, "How did you invest the 10,000 *guilden* I gave you?" The young man began to sing his song, telling in the lyrics the story of how he met the shepherd and gave away his entire fortune to buy this beautiful melody.

The *meshulach* taught everyone the song (for free) and, from then on, all of the Clevelander *Chassidim* would sing the song each week. Then they would dance around the table together and have a wonderful time. I enjoyed watching them too. Often, I used to go to sleep at 3 or 4 a.m.; but that was all right, since there was no school on Sunday anyway.

We also received many important visitors. I was particularly impressed by a certain tall Rav wearing a *spodek.* I later learned that he was Rav Meir Shapiro, the founder of the Daf Yomi Talmud study program, who was in America collecting money for his *yeshivah,* Chachmei Lublin.

The Baker's Daughter

Times were hard in Cleveland during the Depression Years, and staying *shomer Shabbos* was a severe test that many failed. I remember a baker who came to America from Europe and settled in Cleveland. Later his wife came over with their two daughters to join him. One day he brought home his paycheck, and she found out that he had been working on Shabbos! She took the paycheck, threw it in the oven and burned it to a crisp. She told him, "We are not going to eat from being *mechalel Shabbos*!" When he told her that was the only way he could make a living, she decided to buy her own food; she was still not going to eat from his salary.

Her older daughter found a job right away, but the younger one had no luck. She would start a new job every other Monday, but the employers would insist that she work on Shabbos. "If you don't come in on Shabbos, you can forget it," they would tell her. So after a few weeks and excuses, she was unemployed again.

Although an excellent seamstress, she finally was working at the last clothing factory in town. Again she was warned; but, when she woke up that Shabbos morning, she began to cry. No matter what, she just couldn't work on Shabbos. When she showed up Monday morning the foreman yelled at her and embarrassed her in front of everybody, and then fired her. She left crying and continued crying as she walked down the street. Everything seemed over for her.

As she walked along, a young man came over and asked, " Why are you crying? Can I help you?"

"No, no, you can't help me," she said, and she cried even harder.

"I bet you were fired. Was it for not working on Shabbos?"

"Yes, yes, it was."

"Look," he said, "I own a dry-cleaning store, and I am also *shomer Shabbos.* In fact, I am looking for a seamstress. If you want the job you can have it." So he took her in; and it worked out just fine. In fact, she eventually married her boss's *shomer Shabbos* cousin.

The Suit Peddler

I know another couple that was once so poor that there was no food at all in the house. Their seven children were all crying and the wife told her husband to go out and try to sell some of the suits he peddled. "I can't," he said. "All I have left are very short suits and no one will buy them." He didn't have any money left to buy any more merchandise, and he simply didn't know what to do. "Well, we can't just wait to starve," she said. So he put the suits in a suitcase and tried to find some short people on the street.

After walking several blocks, he met, as luck would have it, a particularly tall, husky fellow. The fellow stopped him and asked, "What do you have for sale in that suitcase?" "Suits," he said, "but they won't fit you; in fact, they are all short and small." "Don't worry," said the stranger. "Open up your suitcase and let me have a look." The tall stranger took out a jacket and tried it on — the sleeves came up to his elbow! "Fine," he said, "I know where I can find customers for these suits. How much do you want for all of them?"

They soon made a deal, in cash, and the peddler ran to the grocery store and bought food for his family. With the rest of the money he bought some more suits — the right size this time — and soon he found his business booming. He and his wife eventually used their money to buy a creamery store, where they sold milk, cheese, eggs and such. That is where I met them and heard their story. I believe they eventually became quite wealthy and went into a few other businesses as well.

FIVE

To Europe and Back

The Trip Back to Europe

Mother and I still missed our family, and in the summer of 1929, we went back to Europe for our first visit since we had come to America. I was 10 years old and tremendously excited. Our boat was called *The Bremen* and, like *The Paris,* it was later sunk during the war. Mother and I were the only passengers who ate kosher, so we were given a special little table in the main dining room. Although kosher meat was available, Mother was not sure of the *hashgachah* (supervision); so we lived mostly on sardines, hard-boiled eggs, fruits and vegetables.

We were at sea for about eight days before we landed in Bremen, Germany. Ironically, I particularly remember how polite the people were there. Mother took me to a kosher *milchig* restaurant in Bremen, where I enjoyed the sweet beer they had.

One of mf favorite photographs, Mother and I in Cleveland in 1929, six years after we moved to America

We first visited the mineral water baths at Francisbad where we saw Reb Areleh Belzer, the granson of Reb Shalom of Belz, and at Marienbad, where we saw Reb Yisroel Vizhnitzer. In those days, important *Rebbeim* often visited the baths for their health. Then we traveled on by train to Poland. The Polish countryside was extremely beautiful, a rapidly changing patchwork of fields and trees. We had to change trains in Zeshov. As we finally approached our house in Stryzov, the sun was just about to set. I anxiously looked out the window hoping for a glimpse of my grandmother, aunts and cousins. It had been over three years since I had seen my family; and I missed them all so much.

Together Again

The reunion was very exciting. I was so happy that I burst out crying. Bobeh Yehudis cried too; so we all had a good cry together. Laughing and crying all at once, Bobeh Yehudis asked me, "Where are the diamonds you promised me?" I did not understand what she meant until she reminded me how, when I was leaving for America and she was crying, I had promised to bring her back diamonds from the rich country of America. Of course I was only six then, and I didn't remember anything about it.

It is so terribly sad to know that almost all my family who lived in Poland were murdered. Everything was torn away from them with such vicious cruelty. Their homes and property were all taken away, and then they themselves were killed. But at that time, we knew nothing about the coming Holocaust. It was enough that Mother and I were together again with my sister Leah and the rest of our family. Mother did not want me to have bad feelings about my father, so she sent Leah and me to visit him as well. I was still a little girl, and I remember being afraid that he would try to keep me there with him. I wanted to go back to America with my Mother.

In Stryzov I became friendly with the young daughters of Uncle Chaim Yehudah. I gave them some of the beautiful dresses I had received from a friend of Rav Leifer's in New York (this friend owned a children's clothing store). I remember that my cousins asked me, "Is it true that in America you just pick money up off the streets?"

Then came Shabbos. When I heard Zeide Alter Ze'ev make Kiddush that first Shabbos, I burst into tears all over again. It was so beautiful to be at home with my family. One of my first cousins, Aunt Rochel's son, was a genius at the age of two and a half. I was fascinated by this little boy, who could already make *Kiddush* and who could sing so many different *zmiros* by heart.

Zeshov

The sad part of this visit was that Aunt Rochel developed medical problems and began bleeding profusely. Mother took her to Zeshov, where there was a hospital, but the "specialist" there refused to even examine Aunt Rochel until mother put down $500 in cash! Aunt Rochel did go to the hospital, but the only "treatment" they gave her was strong black coffee (which I understand can help hemorrhaging). *Baruch Hashem,* she recovered, but was weak for quite a while.

I was left behind in Stryzov, and soon became lonesome for my mother. Finally Aunt Fraide, who lived in Zeshov, came and took me back with her. Once we got to Zeshov, Aunt Fraide treated me to lunch in a fancy *milchig* restaurant. She was very surprised because, although the menu was full of various delicacies, all I wanted was bread and butter, a glass of milk and a sour pickle.

Poles and Jews

There had always been pogroms and anti-Semitism among the Polish peasants, but by 1929 anti-Semitism was already growing among the "educated" classes in Eastern Europe. I remember that, on our way home, Mother and I entered a train compartment where two non-Jewish ladies were already sitting. They looked around and said, "Sorry, you can't come in, all the seats are already taken." Thinking quickly, Mother told me loudly in English, "When I get back to America, I am going to tell the government how these Poles treat the Jews." The ladies became frightened because Poland was dependent on American aid between the wars, and they got up and left. We ended up with a compartment to ourselves, but it was a sad omen of things to come.

SIX

Back to America

Massey Avenue

Not much had changed back home in Cleveland, although we did move from Skoville to Massey Avenue, a more Jewish neighborhood. The Skoville house had been a real bargain because the neighborhood was changing, but once my stepfather could no longer find a *minyan* there, we moved.

The Massey Avenue house was smaller. Upstairs, we had only two bedrooms and a large dining room. There was also an office, a little room I used as a bedroom, and a large kitchen. Downstairs was the *shul,* right next door to a big Reform Temple! Believe it or not, the Reform Temple's *shamash* used to come in and visit us often. He still longed for real *Yiddishe* companionship.

School Again

Although I attended public school in Cleveland, I lived a strictly religious life. I even stayed home on *Erev Shabbos* and *Erev Yom Tov* to help my mother prepare for all our guests. I had two kinds of friends. There were my weekday friends, who lived on the same street. We would play jumprope and hopscotch and One-Two-Three O'Leary. Then there were my *Shabbosdik* friends. I was about nine years old and they were older, eleven or twelve. We would get together on Shabbos and talk about the *parshah* of the week and learn *dinim* together.

Since there were no Jewish schools, after public school I was tutored at home in Jewish subjects. Once, I was learning to read from one of the Rebbe's elderly assistants, but he kept falling asleep. Rav Leifer woke him up and said, "Look, she can't say 'Noach' without seven mistakes! You can't sleep when you are supposed to teach my Raichel!"

A Simchah in Waiting

Eight years after her remarriage, Mother was once again expecting a child. Her previous attempts had been unsuccessful, and her doctor didn't give her much encouragement; but she was determined to do everything she could to see it through. She stayed in bed as much as possible and took lots of Vitamin E. In those days, Vitamin E was not available in capsules; instead, I had to buy wheat germ for her at the drugstore.

A Pesach to Remember

That Pesach (1930) was the most interesting one I can remember. Mother had to stay in bed, we had 24 *meshu-*

lachim staying with us, and I was in charge! I had just turned 12. The main problem was not the Pesach cleaning. Mother paid $5 a week to a girl who helped us with that. We used to clean the wall-paper with a special clay bar, which was used as a sponge. The main problem was the enormous amount of cooking to be done for the 27 of us.

The problem was solved when the *meshulachim* got together and said that they would do the cooking themselves! I am not sure that I fully believed them, but we had no other choice. *Erev Pesach* came, and what a sight I saw in our kitchen! The men were all lined up at the sink and at the tables, peeling potatoes and *kashering* chickens. While they worked, they told *divrei Torah* and stories about famous Rebbes, and they sang songs together. This made the work quite pleasant. Actually, I learned from them how to *kasher* chickens.

Then came the final test, the *seder*. Imagine my surprise! The men were very capable cooks and all the food was delicious. We had a beautiful Pesach!

Zeide Becomes Ill

In 1952, just after we moved to America, Reb Alter Ze'ev began to develop a serious case of anemia. He traveled with his son-in-law, Rav Naftali Chaim Halberstam (whose son, Alter Ze'ev, told me this story), and his grandson Rav Ben-Tzion Frankel, to visit a big specialist in Cologne, Germany. He didn't know where to stay in Cologne; but he figured that he could ask someone at the railway station to direct him to the Jewish part of town and handle things from there.

When he got off the train, he was amazed to see an old friend of his waiting there to meet him and take him home! How did this friend know that my grandfather was coming? The Sendyszover Rav, Reb Alter Ze'ev's father, appeared to his friend in a dream the night before and told him, "My son is coming tomorrow on such and such a train, at such and such a time. He is not well and needs to see a doctor. You should go meet him and take him home with you."

When Reb Alter Ze'ev visited the specialist, the doctor told him, "You are quite anemic and need to eat red meat."

"I am sorry," Zeide said, "I eat only chicken."

"Nein. Nein. It must be beef," the doctor insisted.

"What difference could it make?"

"Well, let me put it this way. Just think how you would feel if you were kicked by a cow, rather than by a chicken!"

Despite the doctor's forceful argument, I doubt that my grandfather changed his usual diet — little of anything and almost no red meat. Before he passed away, five years later, he told his children that he now regretted not having eaten more, because it may have affected his health.

The Passing of Bobeh Yehudis

All the years of fasting every day until *Minchah* had made Reb Alter Ze'ev very weak and sick. Bobeh Yehudis was afraid that she couldn't live without him, so she prayed that she should pass away first. Shortly after Chanukah of 1929, she suffered a severe gall bladder attack. While the doctor was preparing an injection for her, my Aunt Rochel began to cry. Bobeh Yehudis, feeling that her end was near, told her,"Don't cry, Rochele. No one has a mother forever."

Rav Leifer learned of Bobeh Yehudis' passing but, since Mother was expecting and not feeling well, he did not tell her. That *Erev Pesach,* Mother became concerned that she had not received a letter from Bobeh Yehudis in a long time. Rav Leifer told her that Bobeh Yehudis had injured her hand, and could not write; but Mother never really believed his story.

In the early evening, before the *seder,* Mother took a nap and had an unusual dream. She saw one of Bobeh Yehudis' friends who told her in Yiddish: "Don't be fooled! Your mother wants you to know that she has been gone for three months now." When Mother woke up, she called Rav Leifer into the room and told him that she knew her mother was gone, while he quietly nodded agreement. When my younger sister was born, Mother named her Chaya Yehudis.

The Inheritance

A few days before that same Pesach (1930), Reb Alter Ze'ev, the Stryzover Zeide, felt that he was going to die. The night before he passed away, he called the family together and personally gave away his special possessions as an inheritance. He especially treasured three things, which he always took with him, even when he was a refugee in Vienna during the war: the cloak of the Chozeh of Lublin, the *tefillin* of the Kozhnitzer Maggid and the cane of his great-grandfather, the Ropshitzer Rav.

To my mother, Rochma Miril, he sent his *sefer Torah* and the cane of the Ropshitzer Rav. I still have his *sefer Torah*; and my younger sister, Chaya Yehudis, the Stroznitzer Rebbetzin, still has his cane. My older sister Leah received a special set of jewelry; but she and all her possessions were lost in the Churban. Reb Alter Ze'ev also gave some jewelry and two candlesticks to my mother. My mother passed on the candlesticks to her sister in Chicago, my Aunt Brucha. One of her grandchildren still has them today.

Towards the end, Reb Alter Ze'ev told his children to bury him in the cloak of the Chozeh of Lublin. He then recited *Shema Yisrael,* said Hashem's Name three times, straightened out his beard, put his hands down, and peacefully passed away. Later, my mother had another dream. This time she saw her father's entire *levayah* (funeral) in full detail. She later met a *Chassid* who was there, and found out that every detail was true. It seemed like a final present to her from her father.

None of us imagined that all these beautiful holy people would leave us. This is the sad part of life. All we can do is to keep our memories of them alive, and remember how much they sacrificed to do *mitzvos* and *maasim tovim.*

Chaya Yehudis

My sister Chaya Yehudis was born at home, because Rav Leifer was afraid that they might mistakenly exchange the baby at the hospital. As it turned out, no one could have made such a mistake. Chaya Yehudis resembled her father, Rav Leifer, very much; she even had his bright red hair.

I was delighted when my little sister was born. She was just like a beautiful doll, with a peaches-and-cream complexion, and reddish-brown eyelashes over bright blue eyes. Once a woman came to Rav Leifer to ask for a *brachah* for children. When she saw Chaya Yehudis, she told him, "I want a beautiful little redhead, just like this one!"

Although Chaya Yehudis was Rav Leifer's natural child, and I was only his stepchild, I never felt that I was loved less. I remember how I once asked Chaya Yehudis to stop making noise, because her father was sleeping. She continued making noise, and I gave her a small slap. Later she ran in crying to her father. "Why did your sister give you a slap?" he asked her calmly. "Because you were sleeping and I was making noise," she answered truthfully. "Well, your sister was right," Rav Leifer said. "You should listen to her."

We Adopt a Grandmother

When Chaya Yehudis was born, an elderly childless widow came to live with us. She was a very pleasant woman and an excellent cook. She used to make our *lokshen* and *farfel* so beautifully that they looked store bought. She also helped Mother with the baby, especially during the week when I was at school.

One day, an elderly widower came to our house and spoke with my parents. He wanted to get married. Mother thought a bit and then talked our widow into marrying him. Unfortunately, she was unhappy at first, because the old man, although he had a lot of money, was extremely miserly. In our home she had become accustomed to cooking and enjoying fine food, but her new husband scrimped on everything. He even bought stale bread for three cents a loaf, when fresh bread cost only six cents. Our "adopted grandmother" came to Mother and complained. Mother called the man in and told him flatly, "Either you treat her right, or we'll take her back!" He promptly changed his ways and I believe they lived happily ever after.

Childless people often asked Mother if she knew of babies they could adopt. Mother would tell them that she couldn't help them find any children, but that she did know plenty of grandmothers and grandfathers they could "adopt"!

The Yiddish Lessons

Around the time my little sister was nine months old, my cousin from out of town came to stay with us for a while. Her mother had traveled to Carlsbad, a famous spa in Europe, to get help for her gall bladder problems. In those days, people believed that bathing in mineral-water springs cured all sorts of ailments (today, most gall bladder trouble is treated with surgery). Rav Leifer hired a woman to teach us both to write Yiddish and other things. She was a precise, neat woman, and careful with her clothing. It was the Depression Years, so she had little black patches that she wove neatly into the fabric of her black satin dress.

I used to practice writing Yiddish by copying Dr. Klorman's correspondence column from the Yiddish newspaper. I remember asking my stepfather, "Why do I have to learn to write Yiddish? It's so difficult to do all this learning after school!" Rav Leifer answered me patiently, on my own level, "Look, when you become a *kallah,* you will need to write to your *chassan* and your *machateniste* in Yiddish."

Learning Chessed

My mother's home was always open, and we had constant company. Every day, when I returned home from school, I went out to buy cakes at Ungar's Bakery for our guests. Around this time I also learned more about how to do *chessed.* It's not always as simple as it seems.

During the Depression Years I was friendly with a family that was truly destitute. The father had a drinking problem, and his seven young children often went hungry. Usually, alcoholism is not a problem among Jewish families; but, unfortunately, this family was an exception. Sometimes, on Purim and before other holidays, Rav Leifer's *Chassidim* would give me a dollar. I would put the money aside and give it to my girlfriend, so her mother could buy food.

Once I was disappointed. I had put together five dollars, which was a lot of money at that time, and had given it to my friend. Instead of buying nutritious food, however, the mother took all her children to the drugstore and treated them to ice cream and banana splits. After that, I no longer gave them money. Instead I would go out and buy bread, eggs, milk and vegetables, so they would have something substantial to eat. I knew how to buy the proper foods, even as a young girl, because I had watched my mother feed her many guests.

Many times I asked my stepfather to help this poor family out, but he didn't always have the money. Once, I told him: "Well, if you don't have money, how about just writing a check?" He thought that was funny. I didn't know that to write a check you have to have money in the bank!

Every time Mother made Shabbos, she sent this same family a basketful of whatever we would be having ourselves: gefilte fish, soup, roast chicken, homemade *challos,* cake, even fruit. Mother sent another big food basket every week to a certain widowed friend who lived alone with her son.

Another time that my *chessed* misfired, it involved a new dress. Rav Leifer had a friend in New York who sold children's clothing, and he always brought me several new dresses whenever he visited us in Cleveland. Once, he gave me some beautiful new outfits, and I used a few for Pesach, while saving my favorite one for Shavuos. Later, when my friends came over to me in *shul,* I saw that one of them had torn her dress. I felt sorry for her, and I gave her my "Shavuos" dress to put on. She went out to play and came back with my new dress all muddy, torn and quite ruined. All one can do is try.

SEVEN

Meshulachim and Meshuggayim

An Open House

My husband and I both grew up in an "open house," and we have always had an "open house" ourselves. This means that people temporarily in need of strictly kosher food and a place to stay could usually come and stay with us for a reasonable amount of time. This was particularly important when we were growing up, because there were few places "out of town" (that is, outside of New York City) where a religious traveler or newcomer could find truly kosher food.

From our earliest childhood, we were constantly surrounded by a flock of *meshulachim* (traveling charity collectors) and — less often but with more impact — *meshuggayim* (mentally ill people).

They were often interesting, sometimes a nuisance, but always an opportunity to practice true *chessed,* without any expectation of thanks or an earthly reward. In short, our childhood was quite different from the average; but we learned a lot about life and about the importance of helping a fellow Jew.

On Meshulachim

Our house almost always had 10 to 20 *meshulachim* staying with us at any one time. They traveled from town to town collecting money for various *yeshivos,* and were allowed to keep a certain percentage of these funds for their own expenses. Some were idealistic, and most were scrupulous about their accounts. Others, as people joked, were just collecting for "Mir Yeshivah" ("my own *yeshivah,*" that is themselves), a pun on the famous European *yeshivah* of that name.

Traveling from place to place, far from the major Jewish centers, living out of suitcases, having to beg for donations and lodging — this kind of lifestyle was not for your typical successful family man. Hardened by their life on the road, some turned out to be rather demanding or — in extreme cases — real characters. On the other hand, all were strictly observant, especially regarding *kashrus,* under the most difficult conditions, and many became close family friends.

Some *meshulachim* were quite special. I remember, for example, Reb Mordechai Erblich, a small man whose face and beard resembled Abraham Lincoln's. Despite his small size, he had a powerful clear voice. I was amazed the first time I heard him, shortly after I was married, because I never expected such a booming voice from such a small man. Reb Mordechai was a Sassover *Chassid* from *Eretz Yisrael,* and he never ate meat during his trips to collect money in America. About all he ate was broiled mackerel, omelets, a parve *cholent* or farina. He was an *erlicher* Yid from an earlier generation, one who used every spare moment to learn or *daven.*

Late one Thursday night, he knocked on my sister-in-law's door. She was bone tired from a full day of cooking and taking care of her little children, and it was terribly hard for her to get out of bed. Finally, she thought of how Reb Mordechai had helped so many others and she said, "For him I really must get up." She pulled herself out of bed just as a brick crashed through her bedroom window, landing right where her head had been. Her answering Reb Mordechai's knock had saved her life!

Meshuggayim

Meshulachim were, by and large, a cheerful, helpful lot, and they rarely stayed more than a few weeks at a time. That was, unfortunately, not the case with our other type of wandering guests, the *meshuggayim.* In the early days there were few public programs or support systems for them. When their families couldn't take it any more, they would try to send them to someone else or just turn them out. *Rebbeishe* houses had more than their share of such guests for a simple reason: Who else had enough *rachmanus* to take them in? Still, I learned the hard way that you must have some limits or you won't have the strength to help all the other people who need you. Three stories, from different periods of my life, are enough for this sad topic. Hashem should send a *refuah* to all such unfortunates.

Reb Chaim S.

A case in point was Reb Chaim S. It all began when my stepfather noticed that on Sunday mornings an elderly gentleman used to visit his Cleveland *shul* and pick up all the cigarette butts on the floor. The man told Rav Leifer that he could not afford to eat, so he used to collect the half-used cigarette butts to have a free smoke and quiet his hunger pangs. In those days (the late 1920s) there was no welfare system to take care of such people; so my parents took him into our home.

To make a living, Reb Chaim, a former *shochet,* sewed uniforms for other *shochtim.* He used to iron these uniforms on our dining room table, each time ruining a different, damask linen tablecloth that my mother had brought from Europe! I asked Mother why she let him do this. Why not give him just one tablecloth to burn? But Mother was afraid of him, and she gave him free run of the linen closet.

One day I came home from school — I was only six or seven — and found Mother sitting on the porch, looking very upset. This was unusual because Mother rarely went outside of the house; she was far too busy. I was even more surprised because, at the time, Rav Leifer was away in New York. "What's the matter, Mama?" I asked.

"Reb Chaim has gone crazy," she said. "He ran after me with a broom and insisted that I sign over the house to his name. When I refused, he threatened to kill me!" She was afraid to go back into the house. What were we going to do? Luckily, just then, two Clevelander *Chassidim* came along, Reb Mordechai Shapiro and Reb Yankele Schreiber, both fine gentlemen. I ran up to them and asked them to help.

"Don't worry, I'll take care of it," said Reb Yankele. He walked up to the front door and yelled upstairs, "Reb Chaim, I hear you have gone crazy and want the Rebbetzin to sign over the house to your name! I am telling you now: if you don't come out and leave in a half hour with your suitcase, I am going to call the police and they will take you away!"

We waited half an hour and, sure enough, Reb Chaim came out, suitcase in hand, and left! I was very impressed by how quickly and efficiently this worked and, years later, when I had to deal with other mentally ill people, I used much the same technique as a last resort.

Rebbetzin R.

Another frightening case involved Rebbetzin R. I met her when I was already 18 years old, just before I left for my second trip back to Europe (1935). She seemed a lovely, knowledgeable lady, with a peaches-and-cream complexion and a blonde *shaitel.* "The Rebbetzin will only be staying for two weeks, until she finds a place for herself," Mother explained. Normally, Mother was unable to take in women guests at all, since we always had a house full of *meshulachim;* but, at the time, Rav Leifer was in Europe again, so Mother shared her own bedroom with her.

When I came back from Europe eight months later, Rebbetzin R. was still there! By this time, she had moved from Mother's bedroom to the attic, where we had a nice guest room with a large window.

Mother had become very depressed and nervous as a result of this woman's stay. She carried around a small, old-fashioned black leather bag, like a doctor's satchel. "She's carrying around a clothesline and a five-pound weight in that bag," Mother told me, "and she has told all the women in the *shul* that I am trying to kill her with them." Obviously, the lady was mentally ill. According to Rebbetzin R., Mother was in conspiracy with the Manischewitz Matzah Company, along with a Rabbi who was a cousin of ours. "If so," people asked her, "why don't you move out?" Rebbetzin R.'s answer was that, as long as she lived with us, she would not be killed; but the moment she moved out, she would be in mortal danger.

As crazy as the story was, several women in our *shul* actually believed it, as did our neighbor, Mrs. Rosenberg, the *shaitelmacher* (wigmaker). It was a horrible proof of how gullible people can be, especially since Mother was well known as a great *baalas chessed.* Finally, I asked Mrs. Rosenberg, "Why don't you take her to *your* house, then?" but she just repeated that Rebbetzin R. said that she could only be safe in our home.

I thought the whole thing was both pathetic and funny. I once asked Mother, "How can people believe all this? She's been here eight months, and she hasn't been killed yet!" Still, Mother was hurt and embarrassed by the woman's terrible stories, and by the people who would come over to her and argue about it. In addition to all the stories she concocted, each day Rebbetzin R. drank four quarts of our expensive *cholov Yisrael* milk and ate eight lemons.

Finally, I decided to help Mother get rid of this "guest." I called

Mrs. Rosenberg and told her that I was going to send Rebbetzin R. over to her house to stay. Then I went to the Police Department and told them the whole story. I told them I don't want this woman to be arrested or hurt. All I want is for the police to come to our house, knock on her door, and say, 'The Leifer family cannot keep you in their house anymore. Mrs. Rosenberg is willing to take you in. Please pack up and leave in a half hour, or else we will come and take you away.' This method, which I had learned from Reb Yankele Schreiber, worked like a charm. A half hour after the policeman's visit, Rebbetzin R. left peacefully with her packed suitcase for Mrs. Rosenberg's!

Years later, when we were living in Los Angeles (1940), we received a worried letter from Belgium, from the daughter of Rebbetzin R. She had not heard from her mother for a long time and wanted us to trace her. We called Mrs. Rosenberg in New York and learned that Rebbetzin R. had begun to go around with her black satchel again. Now she told everyone that her new hostess, Mrs. Rosenberg, was in cahoots with Mother and the rest of the conspiracy to kill her. Her illness apparently took the form of accusing all those who were kind to her. One day, Rebbetzin R. decided to take a train to Washington, D.C. and to complain about "the situation" to President Roosevelt. She obviously never got in to see the President. The White House staffers saw immediately that she was mentally ill and had her admitted to a mental hospital. It was all very sad.

We also learned from Rebbetzin R.'s family that a terrible tragedy had precipitated her mental illness. She and her husband were traveling together by train to a family wedding in Berlin. On the way, her husband received a telegram that his brother had died. He decided to change trains and go back; but, while he was crossing the tracks, he was killed — within sight of his wife — by an oncoming train. Rebbetzin R. had previously stayed with families in Belgium and in London, where she had also accused her hosts of trying to kill her. In these cities, however, Rebbetzin R. had no proper place to stay and would hide out in basements. No one took her in like Mother did in America.

The Difference Between "Help" and Help

Finally, a word or two of *mussar.* Wherever we live, we always seem to find people willing to "help" us do *mitzvos.* That is, they don't actually do things themselves; but they are always glad to find things, often very difficult things, for us to do. We should all be willing to do *mitzvos,* and not just drop them in someone else's lap and walk away.

For example, when I was about 15 and Mother was very ill, a woman friend came over to discuss two elderly sisters who had never married. She wanted these ladies to sleep in our attic in exchange for helping me with the cooking and cleaning. I said right away that I did not want any help, and that I simply could not handle two more guests. Our friend insisted and the sisters move into our attic, and it soon became clear that they were mentally disturbed. They would sit on either side of the refrigerator, in the center of the kitchen, and yell across it, arguing with each other constantly. They also refused to eat, and I was afraid they would starve to death. Finally I explained the situation to Mother and she convinced them to leave.

When Rav Leifer went to Europe, this same friend "helped" us again. She brought us a severely disturbed woman whom she found picking food out of garbage cans! We took her in and put her up in our attic guest room. I prepared a nice bed for her, but I was frightened because she had what seemed to be infected boils on her arms. The next day, I put her sheet right into the garbage can, because I was afraid to put it together with the rest of our laundry. Later, when I asked our friend why she hadn't taken the woman into her own home, she told me, "Oh, *our* family would never take in a vagrant like that!"

They say that a host once asked Rav Yisroel Salanter why he used so little water to wash his hands. He pointed to the orphan girl who had to carry the water to the house and said, "You don't do *mitzvos* on someone else's back." That's a good lesson for all of us to remember.

Other people seem to expect us to "cure" our guests forthwith. Severe mental illness, like severe physical illness, requires lengthy treatment from medical specialists. Non-specialists are simply not equipped to offer the care a mentally ill person needs, just as they are not equipped to do open-heart surgery. One should first ensure that such people get proper treatment. Once they are cured (or almost cured), we should all be willing to help provide for their other needs.

EIGHT

New York

Williamsburg

In 1933, when Chaya Yehudis was three years old and I was 15, Rav Leifer fell ill. He suffered from high blood pressure and frequent nosebleeds, and his doctors told him that the climate in Cleveland was unhealthy for him. We moved to his sister's house in Williamsburg (New York City), where we lived for three years. There was more Jewish life in New York than in Cleveland, but nothing like what there is today.

I loved the big Williamsburg house on South Ninth Street. The basement held an office, a kitchen and a dining room. The first floor held the *shul;* the second, a social hall; and the third, the main family bedrooms. My room was on the fourth floor. The house was roomy, but inconvenient, with many stairs and landings. We shared the house with Rav Leifer's sister and her husband and their entire family, and with Mother's uncle, Reb Osher'l, the youngest brother of Reb Alter Ze'ev. Soon after we moved, Mother became sick, and I had to make Pesach pretty much on my own again.

A Sad Story

Rav Leifer's sister, the Pittsburgher-Nadvorna Rebbetzin, sent us a Jewish woman in her 60s to help me with the Pesach cooking. Unfortunately, this woman hid the fact that she had a severe heart condition because she wanted to make money as a cook. Pesach went by all right; and the lady stayed with us for awhile longer. She slept in my bedroom with me, and from our window we could see the rooftop porches of the neighboring buildings. Late one night, the woman said to me, "Look out there! Don't you see the *Malach HaMaves* (the Angel of Death)!" I looked out, but I didn't see anything, so I assured her that she was just imagining it.

The next day, the woman became very ill; and my mother had one of the *meshulachim* carry the sick woman's bed down to the second-floor reception hall, where we could take better care of her. We brought her special food and whatever else she needed; but later that day I came down and noticed that she was not in her bed.

"What is she doing out of bed? Where is she?" It turned out that our guest had left some money back in her room and, after walking up two flights of stairs to get it, had suffered a severe stroke. Sadly, she passed away a short time later.

The Houseguest Who Married the Shadchan

Half a year later, my mother heard about an elderly lady who had no place to live. She had come to America during the Depression Years and, unfortunately, her son didn't earn enough money to feed both her and his family. He found an interesting "solution." He placed her in a mental institution so that she would be fed! In fact, however, she was not mentally ill.

She was a simple old-fashioned lady, extremely stout, but neat and clean. She lived in our attic. She told me how in the mental home, when Shabbos came, they wouldn't let her light candles, so she would make a *brachah* over the electric lights instead. She also tried not to eat meat there, because it wasn't kosher.

She didn't know how to read. Instead, she would hold her *siddur* upside down and turn the pages. However, she had memorized *Gott fun Avraham,* a beautiful prayer that many women say after Shabbos, and she said this whenever the need arose. One Rosh Hashanah morning I was *davening* near her in *shul.* When all the other people stood up to say *Min Hamaitzar,* just before blowing the *shofar,* I heard her, *nebach,* saying her *Gott fun Avraham* by heart:

ג-ט פון אברהם, פון יצחק, פון יעקב
באהיט דיין פאלק ישראל פון אלעם בייז
אין דיינעם לויב
אז דער ליבער שבת קודש גייט אוועק

G-d of Avraham, Yitzchak and Yaakov,
Protect Your people Israel from all evil,
In Your Praise,
As the Holy Shabbos goes away ...

I didn't know whether to laugh or to cry. But Hashem has *rachmanus,* and I am sure that He accepted her prayer, it was so very sincere.

You must understand that our guests saw themselves as family members, to the point that they would actually begin to get involved in personal family matters. For example, I was 16 years old when this particular houseguest arrived. She promptly decided that it was high time for me to become a *kallah.* I found out when, all of a sudden, some young man I didn't even know telephoned me and asked me out on a date! Our houseguest had taken it upon herself to go to a *shadchan* (matchmaker) and *redd* me a *shidduch*! I explained to the young man that I certainly could not go out on a date without my parents' permission, and that my parents were not at home. I added that, in our circles, boys and girls do not date; we usually meet in our homes. Finally, I was only 16, and still too young for all this!

Later, when the *shadchan* who had arranged the "date" called back, the *meshulach* who answered the telephone began teasing him. I did not want to hurt the *shadchan's* feelings, so I took the telephone and told him to come over and speak to my stepfather about it once he returned home. When the *shadchan* came, my parents made it clear that I was too young for a *shidduch* just yet. They wanted me to wait until I was at least 18.

Then, as it happened, the *shadchan* began to talk about himself. He was now over 70 and wanted to marry. He even had someone in mind ... our houseguest, the same lady who had tried to set up a *shidduch* for me! Rav Leifer gladly arranged everything, and we married the couple off in our own home, with a *minyan* of Clevelander *Chassidim.* As I watched her walk around the *chassan* seven times under the *chuppah,* I thought: We are taught that if you pray for someone else, your own prayers are answered first. This good-hearted lady tried to find a *chassan* for me and, in the process, she found one for herself instead!

Rav Leifer's Brachos

In New York, Rav Leifer continued to give *brachos.* Once a woman who had known him back in Budapest came to ask for his help. She cried as she told him how her husband had lost his job, lived on welfare and then deserted her. She begged Rav Leifer to help her get him back. Rav Leifer gave her a *brachah* and recommended certain special prayers. A few weeks later, her husband returned. Eventually he found a job, and they lived happily together again. Another woman, in a very similar situation, once came to Rav Leifer and asked him to curse her husband, who had left her. He told her: "I am here only to give *brachos.* I can pray that your husband does *teshuvah* and returns to you; but I am not here to curse anybody."

NINE

Europe Again

The Summer of '35

New York City is hot in the summer, and many people go to hotels and bungalows in the Catskill Mountains of New York State. In 1935, when I was 18 years old, I took a summer job as a counselor for the guests' children at a hotel called Gartenberg & Schechter's. This was a *"koch alein"* (cook-by-yourself) hotel. The kitchen was a huge room with separate little stoves, sinks, work spaces and refrigerators, so each woman could do her own cooking. Each family had its own table in the dining room; and there was a little grocery store that took food orders.

I took my little sister Chaya Yehudis to the hotel with me. I enjoyed every minute with her, because I missed my cousins in

Europe so much. One day in July, Mother called unexpectedly and told us that she had arranged things with the Gartenbergs, and that we were to come straight home. We set out for New York City that Friday morning by car; but the car got a flat tire along the way. Chaya Yehudis took it calmly and said, "*Nu*, if we don't get home today, we'll get home tomorrow!" But I told her, "*Chas v'shalom*! We have to get home in time for Shabbos!" We did make it home in time, and Mother told us that she had called us home because my stepfather, Rav Leifer, wanted me to meet him in Europe.

My Second Trip to Europe

Rav Leifer suffered from severe kidney trouble, and he had traveled to Europe to visit the mineral baths at Carlsbad and take the "cure." Then he went to visit his family in Debretzin, Hungary. There he met, and was impressed by, his cousin's son and he wanted me to consider him as a *chassan*.

I took the boat to Europe all by myself and then traveled by train to meet Rav Leifer in Paris. We traveled together to Hungary to meet my prospective *chassan;* but I told Rav Leifer that I was afraid to remain in Europe. Hitler was already very outspoken against the Jews and tempers were rising politically (it was only four years before the Nazi invasion of Poland). Even then I was always interested in world politics. Perhaps I got that from Mother; in Stryzov she used to keep up with the newspapers, so she could report on current events to Rav Alter Ze'ev.

Rav Leifer was sure that the *chassan* would come back with us to America; but I made it a *tenai*: I was prepared to meet him only if he was prepared to emigrate. I never actually met the young man face to face. From a side room, Rav Leifer lifted the gauze curtain and pointed him out, while he was in the midst of a conversation. As it turned out, his mother did not want him to leave Europe, so we never met. Tragically, their whole family was lost in the *Churban*, except for one brother.

My Sister Leah

Rav Leifer went back to Cleveland soon after that; but I stayed on in Europe with my family for another half year or so. I spent most of the time in Sendyshov with my sister Leah. It was surprising how easily I adjusted to living with her once again. We felt an amazing closeness, as if the years had just rolled away and we never had been separated.

Leah had married our first cousin, Aunt Chana's youngest son, Rav Menashe Frankel. He was a big *talmid chacham* and *posek.* People came to him from all the neighboring towns to ask him *she'eilos*; so he did not want to leave Europe and come to America. When Leah got married, Rav Leifer sent her *kest gelt,* just as if she was his own daughter.

My sister Leah Horowitz Frankel and her son, little Alter Ze'ev, both of whom perished in the Holocaust, הי"ד

Young Alter Ze'ev

Leah had a beautiful little boy named Alter Ze'ev, after my grandfather. When I first met him he was around two years old. He was a delightful, bright child with long hair and a lovely lively face. His favorite game was to take a towel and two rolling pins to make a pretend *sefer Torah.* Then he would pretend to be running a *shul,* calling up his uncles and cousins to read the Torah. Little Alter Ze'ev once asked me how I came to Europe. I explained to him how the boat crossed the ocean and how I had passed through many different towns on the way from the port to Sendyszov. I even made a little "map" from items on the table, using the fork for America and the spoon for Europe and so on.

He was such a little *tzaddik* that, at age five, he refused to eat lunch unless his mother also made lunch for his *melamed.* When my cousin Raichel got married, little Alter Ze'ev stood in the kitchen and greeted all the guests: *"Der Rebbe zoll leben a Mazal Tov! Alle Mechutanim a Mazal Tov! Alle chassidim a Mazal Tov und a Mazal Tov!* — To the Rebbe: a Mazal Tov! To all the relatives, a Mazal Tov! To all the *Chassidim,* a great big Mazal Tov!" Then he would sing *Kol Rinah VeYeshuah B'Ohelei Tzaddikim* in a loud voice. When Aunt Chana asked him, "Do you love me?" he told her, "I would love you but, because you're a girl, I can't love you too much!"

When I walked with my little nephew in the street, people would call him *Der Rebbe* because he had an angelic look, as if he were already a rabbi. Unfortunately, he never grew up. When the Nazis took over Sendyszov, the townspeople said they would give up everything they owned if they would just spare this one little boy. My oldest cousin — the Veyelepoler Rebbe, Rav Shloimele Frankel — told me that, of all the terrible losses suffered in the Holocaust, he mourned the loss of this beautiful little boy most of all.

Writing of these beautiful holy people is painful for me. They were all killed for no reason except that they were Jews. This is so hard to come to terms with, especially when you knew them as real living people, as family.

Cousin Raichel's Wedding

While in Europe, I attended the wedding of my cousin Raichel, Uncle Chaim Yehudah's daughter. She borrowed my sister Leah's wedding dress, which was light blue because, in our part of Europe, Jewish brides did not wear white wedding gowns. That was considered a non-Jewish custom. At my own wedding I wore a light-beige gown for the same reason.

The *chuppah* was in front of the *shul* on a Friday afternoon, and the celebration was combined with the Shabbos *seudos.* Before the *chassan* came for the *badeken* ceremony, the custom in Europe was *men bazetzt der kallah,* to sit down with the *kallah.* The women stood around the bride while a *badchan* told her life story and gave her *brachos.* It was all very emotional, especially in my cousin's case, since her mother had passed away just before the wedding. The violin played beautiful sad music, and the *badchan* reminded the bride of all her deceased relatives who would be coming to bless her at her wedding, and everyone had a good cry. In Europe all weddings were a mixture of laughter and tears.

It was impossible to actually feed all the guests, so everyone, except a few out-of-town guests and close family, went home to eat their Friday-night meal with their families. Later, they came back for a large *tish,* a symbolic continuation of their meal with just fruit, light refreshments and *Sheva Brachos.* Even so, we could not seat all the guests at one time, so different guests came for each of the three Shabbos meals and for the *Melaveh Malkah* on *Motzaei Shabbos.* My mother's younger sister Fraide was a very good cook, and she did most of the cooking. I remember seeing the new couple eating Aunt Fraide's golden chicken soup together at the wedding, along with delicious homemade soup nuts. In Europe this soup, *de goldene yoich,* was traditionally the first cooked dish the new couple ate together out of one plate.

At the *Sheva Brachos,* two of the rooms were for the men and the other side of the house was for the women. The men sang *zemiros,* exchanged Torah thoughts and danced the *mitzvah tantz* on Friday night. On *Motzaei Shabbos,* the *badchan* put on a humorous play for the *bachurim.* It was arranged so the women could see it too; and I remember it well.

First, the boys made a stage from two tables. Then the *badchan* told a story about a small town that was having such a hard time that the townspeople could not afford a real Rebbe. Instead, they decided to make their own. They took the shoemaker and taught him how to act like a Rebbe. They dressed him in a long black robe, put a towel over his shoulders to resemble a *tallis,* and told him how to talk to people. Then they started coming to him for help.

His first "case" wasn't all that successful. As it happened, the chimney sweep had fallen down someone's chimney and become a hunchback. Well, the townspeople coached their "Rebbe" on how to give a *brachah* to fix things up; but instead of the chimney sweep, an unexpected visitor arrived out of turn. It was a pregnant woman, who was, of course, another *bachur* dressed up in a shawl. She wanted the Rebbe to give her a *brachah* for healthy children. Remembering his "lines" for the hunchback, the shoemaker-"Rebbe" answered her with the worst possible response: "*Der hoikeh zoll farloren veren und zolst zich keinen oisgleichen!* — That lump should disappear from your body and you should become straight and flat!"

The townspeople later told him the right *brachah* for an expectant mother and wished him better luck next time. Meanwhile the hunchback chimney sweep finally arrived; and the "Rebbe" mistakenly gave him the *brachah* intended for the woman: "*Zolst im ertzihen tzu Torah, l'chuppah umaasim tovim!* — May you keep it and carry it on to Torah, *chuppah* and *maasim tovim*!" In short, the townspeople soon realized that an ordinary person can't be made into a Rebbe by simply changing his outward appearance, a moral worth remembering.

The following day the young couple went to different neighboring towns for the rest of their *Sheva Brachos* celebrations.

The Yomim Tovim

That year I spent Rosh Hashanah, Yom Kippur, Sukkos and Simchas Torah in Sendyshov. The *Yomim Tovim* there were unforgettably beautiful. I can still see all those young men dancing around the table at my Uncle Yosef Chaim's *tish.* They had blond *peyos,* brown *peyos,* black *peyos* — all young, beautiful people, *tahorim.* They are all gone now. I cannot remember the song they were singing. I erased it from my mind, because it would break my heart.

Some people think of the America of that time as rich, and the Poland of that time as poor. In terms of *Yiddishkeit* and *ruchnius,* life in Poland at that time was incredibly rich, and life in America was poor.

Aunt Fraide

After the holidays I visited my Aunt Fraide, the Rozediver Rebbetzin, in Zeshov. She and her husband were very poor and could not afford to both hire a cleaning woman and to give money to *tzedakah.* So Aunt Fraide once told her husband, "I will do the housework myself, and you can pay me the salary a maid would get. Then we can give that money to *tzedakah*!"

Aunt Chana

Finally, I stayed for awhile with Aunt Chana. I helped her make a huge washtub full of soup and bake *bilkes* every Thursday. The whole day we would cook and bake together, and the needy people from the town would come to get hot soup and *challos* for Shabbos. I remember one woman who pinched her little

I spent part of my 1936 trip to Poland with my cousin Baila (right), who perished in the Holocaust

girl to make her cry. Aunt Chana told the woman kindly, "There's no need to pinch her. I will give you plenty of food, just as I give everyone else." I remember that some of these people could not even afford shoes; despite the bitter cold weather, they walked with rags tied around their feet.

One day, the grocery lady told Aunt Chana that she could no longer give her food on credit for the soup kitchen. Aunt Chana promised her that the bill would be paid back in full on Purim, because she knew that her husband had *Chassidim* in America who would be sending her money at that time of year. Aunt Chana asked me several times to help a friend whose daughter was ill, but who was too poor to heat their home.

The Trip Back

From Poland I went to Vienna, Austria, where I stayed with the brother of the Kapitchenitzer Rebbe. His wife was a distant relative of mine, and on Shabbos we all went to the Kapitchenitzer Rebbe's *tish* for *Kiddush* and *cholent.* When the

Nazis took over Austria, my host was sent to one of the first concentration camps. There he was beaten to death.

From Vienna I went to Paris, then Cherbourg, and from there I took the *Queen Mary* home. That was the last time I saw most of my relatives; but I didn't know that as I settled back into my routine in Williamsburg.

TEN

California

Bedford Avenue

When I got back, it was life as usual at our first house in Williamsburg. Finally, Mother could no longer stand the impractical way the house was built, and we moved to Bedford Avenue. I loved our new house, with its flowered rug in the front hallway. The *mikveh* was in the basement, along with an extra side room where the *meshulachim* slept. The next floor housed the *shul;* the floor above, the kitchen and the dining room. Over that was a floor of bedrooms: a large master bedroom, a smaller room for myself and little Chaya Yehudis and another large bedroom for the *meshulachim.* There was also a small kitchenette, where we set up an additional room for guests.

Mother was a big *tzadekes* and, in Cleveland, she used to *daven* with a *minyan* by standing in the room next to the *shul.* In our

Bedford Avenue house, this was too difficult, so she cut a hole in the ceiling of the room where the men *davened,* and sat in the upstairs hall *davening* by the opening. The average passerby would only see another "heating vent" in the floor but, for my mother, it turned that hall into an *ezras nashim* (women's section). It was just one example of what she always taught me, how to turn the ordinary into the holy.

Another Move

Despite his trip to the spa in Europe, Rav Leifer was still sick. His kidneys barely functioned and, in those days, there were no dialysis machines to do the work of kidneys. He was in a bad state, becoming weaker and weaker all the time. He was allowed to eat only *challah,* milk and an occasional piece of cabbage. The doctors would not let him eat protein, because they said he was losing it through his kidneys. They also insisted that he move to a warmer climate.

We wanted Rav Leifer to move to Florida because it was closer to New York; but the doctors said that a dry climate like California's would be much better for his health. He traveled there in 1936 with a friend, one of the *shochtim* from "The Katchkele Club," and, later, Mother traveled to Los Angeles to take care of him herself.

Bais Yaakov

I stayed behind in New York, where I attended the first class of the newly formed Bais Yaakov Teachers' Seminary, taught by Rebbetzin Vichna Kaplan. At last, a real school just for *heimishe frum* young women! I loved every minute I learned there. I remember writing the news of the day on a big piece of cardboard that hung on the bulletin board, and making a large picture of the *Menorah* as it was in the *Bais HaMikdash.* Since both my parents were in California, studying was difficult for me, because I was also responsible for running our entire household. A sizable number of *meshulachim* were living with us, as was my great-uncle, Reb Osher'l, and I had to do all the shopping, cooking, cleaning and laundry.

Mother warned me not to attempt preparing for Pesach by myself that year. She told me to simply leave the house and stay with our neighbors. Some of the *meshulachim,* however, insisted that I make Pesach at home anyway; they said that it would be too difficult for Reb Osher'l to leave the house. I tried to make Pesach at home, but it was too much for me. We even had to keep live carp in the bathtub! One of the *meshulachim* helped me cut up the fish, but the job was tiring and tedious. Worse, this same *meshulach* quarreled with our janitor, who left us. That meant that I had to do the heavy cleaning work myself and, since I already had chronic bronchitis, I soon became very ill.

To California

Poor Mother had to stop caring for Rav Leifer in California and rush back to New York City to take care of me! After one look, she decided to take me back with her to Los Angeles to join the rest of the family. Although I missed Bais Yaakov terribly, I was totally overwhelmed by the housework in New York, and I really had no choice. Years later, when my younger sister, Chaya Yehudis, went to study in the New York Bais Yaakov, Rebbetzin Kaplan told her that I had been one of her best students.

Mother asked a good friend to take care of our New York home, and asked another family to take care of the bills. When we returned to New York the following year, Mother rented our part of the house to a very nice woman, who kept it very well over the years. The *shul* on the middle floor paid part of the heating bill, and the income from the *mikveh* paid the mortgage.

Things were difficult for us in Los Angeles. Some people in other *shuls* were worried that Rav Leifer, who was very gifted, would be unfair competition, so our rented apartment soon became "unavailable." We then lived in a variety of rented houses while we looked for a place to settle down. In our second rented house, a very interesting thing happened to me.

Mrs. Kash

Before Purim, a woman named Mrs. Kash came to ask Rav Leifer for a *brachah.* She had to have an operation and her surgeon, a well-known expert, practiced only in a Catholic hospital, which had non-Jewish statues in every room. Mrs. Kash, of course, felt very uncomfortable about the statues, but she was afraid to go to another doctor. Rav Leifer suggested that she simply look away from them.

I woke up one Purim morning with the strangest dream still in my mind. Mrs. Kash was looking at a statue and feeling very frightened. It reminded her of so many thousands of Jews who had suffered so much in the name of that same cross. In the dream, she started to cry. I came into her room, put my arm around her and reassured her. I told her: "Just ignore those things. Everything will be all right. You will be fine, you will go home and everything will be O.K." In the morning, I told Mother about my dream while we were busy preparing for the Purim *seudah.*

In the middle of the *seudah,* the doorbell rang. A young woman came in and told us that she was Mrs. Kash's daughter. Her mother had had the very same dream the night before! Mrs. Kash sent a donation for the *shul* with her daughter and, *Baruch Hashem,* she completely recovered from the operation. When I later told my mother-in-law about this remarkable double-dream, she thought that the whole thing might have been a fantasy. Years later she went to a wedding and met Mrs. Kash herself, who told her the whole strange story.

Boyle Heights

Eventually, we bought a house of our own in Boyle Heights, and set up our own *shul.* The *minyan* was held in the living room, and the women's section was in the dining room. The bedrooms were upstairs, and there was a small additional bedroom downstairs, so Rav Leifer could lie down whenever necessary. I spent most of my spare time helping take care of Rav Leifer, who was very ill. During the week I also went to night classes in English and, on Sundays, I visited friends of my mother who lived nearby.

Rav Leifer was always very considerate of me, especially in his last years. For example, although I was only 20, he asked for my opinion about how to remodel the kitchen to make it more convenient. Once, he walked in while I was giving my little sister supper (I had broiled a small chicken for her). He complimented me so nicely to my mother: "Isn't it wonderful the way she is taking care of our little child, making sure that she has everything she needs?" Each week I used to set out a change of Shabbos clothes both for him and for Mother, and he would say appreciatively, "See how she takes such good care of us."

The Esrogim

Despite Rav Leifer's illness and our other problems, we continued to run an open house for *meshulachim* and other guests. Most were from New York or other American cities, but some were from Europe or even *Eretz Yisrael,* then called Palestine. I particularly remember two *meshulachim* who were our last link with the Jews of Israel during World War II. Life was very difficult there, and these two *meshulachim* had decided to come to America and sell Israeli *esrogim* to get the money they needed to support their families.

Traveling westward through Europe was impossible because of the war, so they headed eastward. They went by caravan overland to Baghdad, and then flew to Karachi and Calcutta (then part of the British Empire). From India they went by boat to the West Coast, a long rough journey on which they ate only the black bread, matzah and herring they had brought along. They looked like exhausted prisoners when they arrived at our house in Los Angeles. Then they took a four-day train ride to New York City, where they were able to sell their *esrogim* for a good price. Later they told me that they took the last Swedish boat from the American West Coast back to Asia, just days before the Japanese attacked Pearl Harbor and America entered the war in December 1941.

The captain, although Swedish, was anti-Semitic, and their trip back was even harder than their trip over. Worse, when their plane landed in Baghdad, the pilot announced, "All passengers going to Lod Airport (Palestine) please disembark; we are not flying on to Lod." Iraq had revolted against the British, and the plane was being conscripted by the authorities to take British civilians back to safety in India. The two *meshulachim* were taken off the plane and just left there on the tarmac — "Europeans" and Jews stuck all alone in enemy territory. I asked them, "What did you do?" They said, "*Vas ti'en tzvei Yiddin? Men zogt Tehillim!* — And what do two Jews do? We recite *Tehillim!*" They also recited the old prayer אלקא דר' מאיר ענינא. All of a sudden, the pilot ran out waving a telegram saying that they could fly on to Lod after all. They arrived at noon, and even made it back to Yerushalayim in time for Shabbos. Unfortunately, few other stories from that era had a happy ending.

The Last Illness

Although we were in California, a land of sunshine and blue skies, we often felt deeply depressed because of Rav Leifer's illness. His kidneys hardly functioned, and he had to visit the hospital frequently for blood transfusions. We knew that he was living on borrowed time; but it was terrible seeing him so weak.

Even then, Californians knew a lot about nutrition and diet. I remember the beautiful vine-ripe fruits and vegetables I saw there whenever I went shopping; even the fish was gorgeous, delicious and inexpensive. We finally decided to use natural-diet doctors as well as our regular ones, although none of them thought that Rav Leifer had more than three months to live. They were amazed that we were able to help keep him alive for almost another five years, with constant care and a diet free of uric acid. He had his ups and downs; but occasionally, when he felt up to it, he would still see people and help them as a Rebbe. Even now, when people come to ask me for advice regarding illness, I tell them to talk to their doctors about diet and nutrition as well.

Rav Leifer would often ask: "Why are you making such a fuss over an old man?" and Mother would answer, *"Du bist di kron fun mein kopf* ... You're the crown of my head. What am I going to do after you leave me?" He used to tell her: "Raichel will take care of you." It was heartbreaking to hear him talking that way, but he was very ill and he could see the handwriting on the wall and accept it. This amazed me. I have met a lot of sick people in my time, but not everyone can accept the truth about their difficult medical situation.

Towards the end, he had to have an oxygen tent, and the thermostat had to be watched constantly, and turned higher or lower by hand. Mother and I took turns. I watched the thermostat from 12 midnight to 5 a.m.; then Mother would take over and I would sleep until late morning. Then I would study, read and go in every so often to check the thermostat, so Mother could get some rest. It was hard work, but we did it lovingly.

The last Friday night of his life, he tried to hold his *becher* and make *Kiddush* in bed. It was very hard since his hands were shaking from the uric acid that was poisoning his system. Finally he said, as if speaking to someone we couldn't see, *"Loz mir machen Kiddush* — Let me make Kiddush." His hands continued shaking, but he did make *Kiddush,* just as he had wanted. Rav Meir Leifer, the Nadvorna-Clevelander Rebbe, passed away three days before Pesach 1941. I learned a lot from him; he lived only to do *mitzvos* and *maasim tovim.*

Another Hard Pesach

That Pesach was a hard one, both emotionally, spiritually and physically. While my mother and sister were sitting *shivah,* I had to make Pesach again for all our family and guests. This was quite a job, although four *meshulachim* and a lady who was spending Pesach with us helped. Fortunately, I had a lot of experience from the year (1930) that I had watched the *meshulachim* do it.

A Last Cure

Shortly after Rav Leifer had passed away, a woman came to our house to see him. Mother told her that the Clevelander Rebbe had passed away, and the woman told us a story about how he had helped her. Her sister had once been ill in the hospital, bleeding profusely from her gums. The doctors had tried everything, but they could not stop the bleeding. They had given up, saying that she would probably bleed to death. Rav Leifer advised the woman to put iron nails into an apple, bake it and feed the soft apple to her sister. She did, and her sister recovered.

I Save Our Home

A week after the *shivah,* I heard one of the men from the *shul* say, "She's a widow, what does she need the house and the *shul* for anyway?" It seemed to me that some of the *baalabatim* might be planning to take over our house. They could actually have done this since, although the house had been bought with Rav Leifer's money, he had officially registered the building in the name of his congregation.

In June 1941, I was just visiting Boston. After our marriage, the Rebbe and I moved back there to live.

The next day, I telephoned the lawyer who had helped Rav Leifer buy the house. I asked how to protect Mother, so that no one could take the house away from her. The lawyer told us to take out a large second mortgage on the house, so whoever tried to sell it would have to pay off that mortgage first. We quickly wrote out the required papers and thus assured Mother her home; but we were still left with the large first mortgage to pay off.

Of course, these personal events were only part of our sorrow. Europe was at war, and its beautiful Jewish communities, the product of generations of effort and suffering, were being destroyed.

ELEVEN

The War Years

Wounds

This part of my family's history is hard for me to discuss. The family we left behind in Europe was extremely close to me. They were not mere statistics or history. They were my sister, my aunts and my little nephew Alter Ze'ev, playing with his Torah scroll of towels and rolling pins. You won't find any of that in the encyclopedias or history books. It is all too sad and painful; and I will tell you just a little about some of my family, those you know best.

My Father

My grandfather, Rav Yehudah Ungar, the Sokolover Rebbe, passed away only three months before the beginning of World War II; and my father, Rav Naftali Ungar, took his place in Neimark. When the Nazi troops arrived, they found him learning Torah, with great *mesiras nefesh,* in a makeshift *yeshivah* on the top floor of a factory building. The Nazis shot him, and all of the men with him, dead. My father was buried in a mass grave with all the others. His murderers never even knew who he was.

My Sister Leah

When Mother and I left for America in 1924, my older sister Leah stayed to take care of Bobeh Yehudis and Reb Alter Ze'ev. Although I was separated from Leah when I was about five, we remained very close. I visited her in Poland when I was eight and again when I was 18. It is painful to tell you how hard we tried to bring Leah over to America when the Nazis came to power in Europe.

At one point Leah actually went to the Polish Consul to apply for a visa. When the officials asked her what she planned to do in the United States, she said that she planned to work there. She thought that this would help her case (people were always trying to guess what the authorities wanted). Unfortunately, a Polish citizen could only go to America on a visitor's visa, not on a work permit; so her request was denied.

When she was about 17, Leah married her cousin, Rav Menashe Frankel, a fine young *talmid chacham,* and Rav Leifer had sent her a dowry of $3,000 which was a huge sum in those days. Mother had just given birth to Chaya Yehudis, so she could not travel to Poland for Leah's wedding. After that, it was impossible for Leah to leave without her husband and children. Later, when things got much worse, Rav Leifer got out of his sickbed to fill out special papers, in a last attempt to bring her and her family to America. Sadly, just when it seemed possible that they might escape, her son, little Alter Ze'ev, had an appendicitis attack and was rushed to the hospital. Leah refused to leave his side.

Leah's husband, Rav Menashe Frankel, was deported by the Russians as soon as Hitler marched into Poland. They caught him as he tried to escape, with a small bundle of his things in one hand

and a suitcase containing a *sefer Torah* in the other. The Russians sent him to Siberia. He survived that terrible winter, but on Pesach, he couldn't bring himself to eat the *chametz* that was available. He tried to survive by eating only the scraps of sugar that he could find, and eventually died from starvation. Leah, little Alter Ze'ev and his sister Yehudis were all killed by the Nazis, *yimach shemam.*

Later I had a dream in which Leah was being sent to her death by the Nazis. I saw her going up in smoke to *Gan Eden* — even though we didn't know about the crematoria in those days — and I cried out to her, "Don't leave me!" But all she could say was, "Do I have a choice?"

An American English Lesson

My grandfather Reb Alter Ze'ev's youngest brother, Reb Osher'l, did come to America; and he lived with us in Williamsburg. He was panicked by the situation in Europe and tried as hard as he could to get his wife and children out by becoming an American citizen. Unfortunately, as hard as he tried to learn English, he never quite mastered it. The judge, who heard his citizenship case, did not like the way he answered the questions and sentenced his whole family to death, just because his English wasn't good enough. I had met his family on my second trip to Europe.

In those days, American "morality" included judges who would let innocent women and children be killed if their relatives didn't speak English well enough. This is especially painful when today immigrants, without a word of English, only have to raise their right hand to become citizens. There is a lot of talk today about the loss of morality in America and "when did America lose its soul?" For me, it was when people forgot that "saving a life is like saving a whole world."

Whenever I go to visit my mother's grave, I visit Reb Osher'l's grave as well. I light a *yahrtzeit* lamp for him, and I often have him in mind when we say the *Yizkor* prayers. He once said that on the day of his funeral all the Jews would wear *shtriemlach* and be in a happy mood. People didn't understand what he meant until he passed away — on Purim.

Aunt Chaya

My great-aunt Chaya was one of Reb Alter Ze'ev's oldest sisters. I visited her in Poland in 1935, when she was about 93 years old. She was still intelligent and clear headed, and had the beautiful smooth skin of a young woman.

When the Nazi S.S. squads came to her town to gather all the Jews, she must have been almost 100 years old. What on earth could the Nazis want from a 100-year-old woman? Still, they sent her to Auschwitz. Later, I met a woman who had been with her on the train. She told me that Aunt Chaya turned to her and gave her an amazing *brachah*: that everything in her life should turn out all right. She told her, "I want you to know that whenever you are in an *eis tzarah* (a time of trouble), you should mention my name, Chaya bas Rochel, and Hashem will see you through all your troubles."

This woman suffered through all the misery of the Holocaust and somehow survived. Whenever anything went wrong in her life, she would mention the name of my great-aunt, Chaya bas Rochel. She must have mentioned her name again years later, when she came to Boston regarding a serious heart condition, because the specialists there gave her a clean bill of health.

Aunt Malka

Of Reb Alter Ze'ev's eight daughters and one son, only three daughters survived the Churban in Europe. My mother went to Cleveland and her sister Brucha went to Chicago. Aunt Malka and her family were shipped to Siberia and managed to survive despite incredible suffering.

Aunt Malka married Rav Naftali Chaim Halberstam, the son of the Gorlitzer Rav. They lived with their four daughters and one son in Gorlitz until the Russians deported the whole family to Siberia during the war. Aunt Malka never spoke to me about the war years; but she once told my mother about it. On the very first day that they arrived in the freezing cold of Siberia, the Russians put them to backbreaking work, chopping down trees to build their own huts. Her husband, unused to such heavy work, had a heart attack and died that very first day in Siberia.

Cold, hungry, overworked and alone, Aunt Malka and the children suffered greatly. At one point, all of them came down with typhus and almost died. Later, they all became severely ill from eating giant melons, the only food they could find. The winters were terrible. They had no furniture and had to sleep on the wooden floor. In the morning, their hair would stick to the wood from the frost.

Aunt Malka's eight-year-old son Alter had to drive a horse and buggy. She used whatever crumbs of oats that were left over in the horse's feedbag to make a weak oat soup for her children. Once, the horse fell into a ditch, and her son was afraid that he might be killed since, in Siberia, a horse was considered more valuable than a human being.

Somehow, they all survived the war. Despite the awful conditions in Stalin's labor camps, many Jews survived Siberia because they were not murdered outright. Actually, people say that Stalin killed more people than Hitler; he just didn't discriminate.

When the war was over, Aunt Brucha arranged for Aunt Malka and her children to come to America. They stayed with us for quite a while, until they were able to find an apartment of their own. Aunt Malka's children and grandchildren all became prominent Rabbis and Rebbetzins (one is married to the Tchenchkovitzer Rav of Brooklyn).

Public Indifference

The indifference of most "moral" Americans during the *Churban* (Holocaust), Jews and Gentiles alike, was too awful to discuss. It was not just the refugee ships turned back, the visas denied and the hypocrisy of the officials. It expressed itself in hundreds of smaller ways as well.

I remember when the Germans invaded Poland in 1939. We were still living in Los Angeles and were worried sick about our family in Galicia. Our next-door neighbor, who was Jewish, said, "Why are you carrying on so? Europe is thousands of miles away; you are safe here." I tried to tell her about my relative, the brother of the Kapitchenitzer Rebbe in Vienna. When the Nazis took over Austria in the Anschluss, they had sent him to one of the first concentration camps, I believe it was Dachau, and beat him to death. Now they had all of Poland. "What about the three million Jews who are still trapped there?" I asked her, but she couldn't feel concerned.

Later, after Pearl Harbor, she came over to apologize and to ask us to pray for her husband who was going over to fight Japan. It is such a sad part of human nature. We so often worry only about ourselves, and always think it can not happen to us.

In 1943, there was a big Rabbis' March on Washington during which over 200 Rabbis begged the U.S. Government to do something — anything — to help stop the slaughter of the Jews in Europe. Although the Rebbe and I were just married, and he had received his *smichah* only a short while before, he was invited to join the many other important *Rabbanim* on the March. He came back deeply disappointed. Despite the terrible urgency, President Roosevelt was "too busy" to even see them. In general, no one really seemed to care how many Jews died. So much for American concern, even as late as 1943.

The Museum

Now I see that people are busy building Holocaust Museums. Hitler, *yimach shemo,* also wanted to build a Holocaust Museum, in Prague, his Oesthauptstadt. What could that same concern have done in 1943? What could all those millions of dollars do now for our *yeshivos* and Talmud Torahs? Our job is not to give *Yiddishkeit* a decent burial; it is to keep it alive. The *kadoshim* of Europe wanted to live and to serve Hashem. We must live for them and restore what was lost.

I know that this is impossible to do completely. Still, when I see all our college-educated *baalei teshuvah* and their children, and now their grandchildren, sitting around the Rebbe's Shabbos *tish* in *bekeshes* and *shtriemlach,* singing and discussing Torah, I realize that ultimately the *Rebbeim,* not Hitler, won.

TWELVE

Shidducim

On Shidduchim

A Jewish marriage is very special, since it involves choosing a lifetime partner and raising a Jewish family. It is one of the most serious decisions one can ever make. It never ceases to amaze me how some people carefully plan buying a house or a car — asking family and experts for advice — and yet get married pretty much all by themselves. What can one expect from a chance meeting between two people who have had no previous experience with married life or raising a family? All they know is that they enjoyed going to movies and restaurants together for the last three months! It is an example of Hashem's great *rachmanus* that such marriages turn out as well as they do.

In Chassidic circles, marriage is very much a family affair. Customs vary, but a typical "American" *shidduch* might go something like this. When the parents feel that their son or daughter is of age, they let it be known that they are ready to *"redd a shidduch."* They discreetly make this known to Rabbanim and Rebbetzins, relatives and friends. Occasionally they also approach professional *shadchanim*. Soon suggestions start flowing back to the family. Brothers suggest their friends at *yeshivah,* or their friends' brothers; married sisters suggest their brothers-in-law; *Roshei Yeshivah* suggest their students; neighbors suggest their nephews, and so on.

The parents discuss each possibility in turn, weeding out the majority who just don't fit their daughter. They then "zero in" on one special candidate and start collecting all the information they can on him, making calls and asking questions. Such investigations are usually quite thorough. Then the girl's parents go to meet the boy and his parents. If things seem all right on both sides, the boy and girl meet.

The first meeting is usually at the girl's home. Both families are usually present, although the couple may talk by themselves for awhile in another part of the room. Similar backgrounds and future plans are important considerations, as are overall impressions. Afterwards, both young people go home and talk things over with their "advisors": parents, married sisters and friends. All angles are discussed and considered, over and over again. Unless something was obviously wrong, there is usually another meeting and then another. If the young person finally decides, "He's just not for me," they start all over again with candidate number two. Ideally there is no coercion, and it is rare for the first *shidduch* to be "Mr. Right." On the other hand, with such careful screening by the parents, three or four candidates usually does it. The parents then discuss the *tanaim,* the financial and other responsibilities that each family undertakes. The proposed engagement is made public at a happy celebration called a *vort.*

College girls tell me that the non-*frum* world is now going back to this system using computers. Students fill out forms saying who they are and what they are looking for. The computer matches people with similar interests. Although perhaps a step forward, this still falls far short of the "old-fashioned" *shidduch* system. For one thing, a few short questions do not seem much to base a whole life on. So what if they both like pasta and classical music? Secondly, the computer hasn't known the girl since she was a child, never cried every time she had a cold, and really doesn't care what happens to her. In short, I was glad that I had my family's help through it all.

My Turn

During the first half year after Rav Leifer's passing, my mother did not do anything about *shidduchim* for me. After Rosh Hashanah and Yom Kippur, she told me it was time to start thinking of such things, so we traveled back to New York.

On the way, we stopped over with friends in Chicago, where Mother had arranged for me to meet a certain young man. When the appointed time came, however, he didn't show up. Mother was very upset; but I just said, "He is obviously not my *shidduch, gam zu l'tovah* (This too is for the best)." I was already 23, and he was only 18 or 19, which I felt was too young for me.

In New York, Mother arranged for me to meet many different *shidduchim*. She first went to investigate them; and I met the young man only if she felt that he was an appropriate candidate. Once I met with a young man and asked him if he would keep an open house, as my parents had done, after we got married. He said that he didn't like the open house idea very much, and I knew at once that he was not for me.

I Save Our House Again

In New York we lived in the apartment on the top floor of our former *shul*. We were there for only a few days when we received a letter telling us that our house was going to be sold at the next Sheriff's Sale! I called the mortgagee, but she said that she had nothing to do with it and advised me to get in touch with the bank manager. Mother wanted to telephone the man we had left in charge of paying our bills, the son of her best friend. "Don't bother calling him," I told her. "If he was planning to sell our house at the

Sheriff's Sale without telling us, that means he didn't pay our bills. We had better investigate what is going on here." That was the first time I ever had a real disagreement with my mother; but I remembered what had happened in Los Angeles, when I also had to save our home.

I went to see the bank manager, who explained that the man we had left in charge of the house had never paid the mortgage, not even the interest! I asked the bank manager how much he thought he could get for the house at the Sheriff's Sale and he said $4,000 (the house had originally cost $7,000). I offered to buy the house myself at that price. I was able to get a loan of $1,000 from my great-uncle to use as a deposit; and I promised the bank manager that we would soon pay the rest.

Although we were terribly disappointed, we never said anything to the man who had never paid our bills. Once, while we were at his mother's house, a certain *chazan* came in and said to the son, "What's with that house on Bedford Avenue that was supposed to be sold at the Sheriff's Sale? You were supposed to get it for me for $2,500!" My mother and I just looked at each other sadly and didn't say a word to her friend. Her son didn't have any money, and we didn't want to hurt her feelings.

The Mikveh Lady

You might not think that a pile of hidden towels would have much to do with my *shidduch,* but it did. When we left New York for Los Angeles in 1936, we left a certain lady in charge of the *mikveh.* A laundry service brought and cleaned the sheets and towels. Once we returned to New York, Mother and I lived upstairs, where we had nothing to do with the *mikveh.*

One day the man taking care of the *mikveh's* bills came upstairs and said, "The laundry service complained that they are missing towels and sheets. I want to check if you are using any upstairs." I told him, "Absolutely not! Why should we use the linen from the *mikveh*?" In fact, the *mikveh* sheets were square and too small for a bed, so we had no possible use for them. The man insisted that the linen was missing, and that the *mikveh* lady didn't know where they were. "Well," I said, "she takes in help to clean, maybe somebody put the missing linen away somewhere."

We went downstairs and looked through all the closets in the *mikveh,* but they were bare. Finally, I suggested that maybe one of the workers had hidden the linen in the large trousseau trunk that sat in the hallway. Sure enough, when we opened the trunk, we found it piled high with sheets and towels!

Once the secret was out, the *mikveh* lady felt so guilty that she began yelling at me, although I had never accused her of hiding the linen herself. Anyway, she left her job at the *mikveh* and we had to find someone else to take her place. Worse, despite the Torah's prohibition against such things, her husband held a grudge against us.

Slander and Death

The first person who suggested a *shidduch* with my future husband, the Bostoner Rebbe, Rav Levi Yitzchak Horowitz שליט"א, was a *meshulach* who had known me since I was a little girl in Cleveland. This *meshulach* moved to New York and later became a diamond merchant and a *Chassid* of the first Bostoner Rebbe, Rav Pinchas Dovid Horowitz. This *meshulach* told Rav Pinchas Dovid and his Rebbetzin, Soroh Sashe, that I would be the best possible *shidduch* for their son. My mother, who was in New York at the time, met with Rav Pinchas Dovid and they both agreed that the *shidduch* seemed very suitable, although I was slightly older.

On a Thursday, the seventh day of Kislev, Rav Pinchas Dovid was visited by the husband of our former *mikveh* lady. When this man heard that the Rav had practically agreed to my *shidduch,* he strongly advised against it. He said, for example, that I was an old maid who would never have any children. (The Rebbe and I have had, *Baruch Hashem,* five children, numerous grandchildren and are now welcoming great-grandchildren!)

The Rebbe's father, blind and suffering from a heart condition, was in a quandary. Here he had practically made an agreement with my mother, and he certainly did not want to embarrass me. Still, he was now hearing terrible things about me, from a man who supposedly knew me well. As a true *tzaddik,* he somehow couldn't believe such lies were true; but still the man had clearly said ...

He never told his Rebbetzin about this conversation and instead struggled with his thoughts all alone that night. He never had to give his decision. That very night he suffered a heart attack and passed away before dawn.

That *Motzaei Shabbos* I was supposed to take the train for a four-day, three-night journey to New York to meet the Rebbe's family (in those days, you didn't just fly). Mother called and told me to come a month later than we had planned; but she didn't tell me why. Later I learned from the Jewish newspapers that Rav Pinchas Dovid had passed away. During the *shivah,* the man who had slandered me felt very guilty. He approached Rebbetzin Soroh Sashe and told her the whole story. He added that he was sorry. It was all terribly sad.

Meanwhile, back in Los Angeles, one of the *meshulachim* learned that Mother wanted me to come to New York to meet my future husband. He advised me not to go. He told me that the young man was *"ze'er mius and azoi klein az er ken gain shpatziren unterin tish!* — very ugly and so short that he could go for a walk under the table!" Several months later, after I had met the Rebbe in New York — he couldn't walk under any table I know — and we had become engaged, I returned to Los Angeles. I was angry at this *meshulach* and asked him, "How could you lie to me? My *chassan* is a fine tall fellow and quite good looking!" He answered, "I didn't like your mother-in-law, so I felt I should break up the *shidduch.*" I just couldn't understand people doing things like that.

The First Meeting

After the *shivah,* the Bostoner Rebbetzin said that she still wanted the *shidduch,* since her husband had wanted it before he passed away. So, about a month later, I went to New York after all.

My mother invited all of their family over to our top-floor apartment. The Rebbe, his mother, older brother, younger sister and a nephew all came. We sat around the dining room table while the Rebbe and I talked. We found that we had similar backgrounds. We had each grown up in the home of "out-of-town" Rebbes (everything outside of New York was "out of town" in those days), with all the difficulties, loneliness and peculiarities that implied. We had each grown up in the same surroundings: an open house, complete with *meshulachim, orchim,* a *mikveh,* a *shul* — all the usual "necessities" of a *Rebbeshe* home. We each had similar hopes and plans.

That evening the Rebbe spoke very little; his mother and older brother did much of the talking for him. Afterwards, I told Mother that I thought that he was very nice, but that I wasn't sure. Perhaps he was too young for me or perhaps he was too shy. Mother reassured me that, in his own home, he was quite friendly, and that he had an excellent sense of humor (he still does). "I've seen quite a few young men," she said, "and he's the nicest of them all. They have an open house like we have, and they share things like our family does."

Advice

One of my older cousins also advised me in favor of the *shidduch.* He insisted that the *chassan's* being a bit younger would not be a problem. "Most of my sisters married younger husbands," Mother agreed, "and they all had very happy marriages."

This was quite true. For example, Aunt Chana was 15 when she married her husband, who was only 13 (people married a lot earlier in Europe than in America). Mother's Aunt Zipporah was 19 when she married her husband, who was 15; Aunt Brucha was also six years older than her husband. In fact, I was sort of following a family "tradition." Furthermore, as both my mother and my mother-in-law realized, in those days there weren't that many *Rebbeshe mishpachos* in America. Still, I wasn't quite sure what to do. I was young and the decision was very difficult for me.

That night, I had a dream. My stepfather, the Clevelander Rebbe came back to see me and said simply, "This is your *zivug* and you should accept the match. I have a beautiful *Pesachdik* wine bottle and a heavy silver tray. Take these two special, lovely things and give them as gifts to the *chassan*." And so we arranged a second meeting for the whole family.

The Second Meeting

The Rebbe's father was a Yerushalmi and his mother was born in Tzfas so, naturally, the Rebbe always dreamed of

The Rebbe, Shlita, and I have been married now for over 50 years; and every day brings us new reasons to be grateful to Hashem

returning to *Eretz Yisrael*. Whenever *shidduchim* were seriously considered, he would ask them if they would agree to live in *Eretz Yisrael*. They would always say that they wanted to live near their parents in New York. As you must have guessed by now, I was far more independent than that.

At our second meeting, the Rebbe asked me that very same question. Would I go with him to live in Israel? Remembering my mother's marriage to Rav Leifer, which meant leaving her entire family in Europe to come to America, I said simply, *"Mit ah mahn, geit min me'eiver layam* — With a husband, a woman goes over the sea." When he heard that, he too decided that I was his *zivug*.

A few weeks later we got engaged. We stayed engaged for a full year, so that the wedding could take place after the Rebbe's year of mourning for his father.

The Kapitchenitzer Rebbe

When I became a *kallah*, my mother went with me to see the Kapitchenitzer Rebbe. He asked me whether my husband would become a Rebbe in Boston, Los Angeles or Williamsburg. I said that I did not know which my husband was going to choose. The Kapitchenitzer Rebbe asked me, "Which do you want him to choose?" I answered, "Whatever he decides is good enough for me. I am not going to tell him what to do. *B'ezras Hashem*, everything will work out fine."

The Kapitchenitzer Rebbe then turned to Mother and told her that I would have a good marriage. "How do you know?" she asked. "Well," he said, "if she's happy with whatever her *chassan* is going to do, there aren't going to be any problems!" The Kapitchenitzer Rebbe also came to our *chassanah* (wedding).

A Trip to Boston

We later had a second big engagement party in June, this time for the Bostoner community in Boston. Rebbetzin

Soroh Sashe had a dear friend, Mrs. B., who lived in Boston's West End, where the engagement party was held. She insisted on my being her guest, and she put me in the spare bedroom that was usually used by *meshulachim.*

That night, I woke up with a bad sore throat and started to feel itchy all over. I said to myself, "What kind of *kallah* am I?" I turned on the light and saw that the sheet was covered with bedbugs! They were crawling over everything, including me. I was horrified and tried to shake myself off. I didn't know what to do. Finally, I put on my robe and went to the living room to telephone Rebbetzin Soroh Sashe. Meanwhile, Mrs. B's older daughter heard that I was up. When I explained the problem, she made up a bed for me on the couch. That wasn't bad; but the next morning, I changed homes. I remained very friendly with Mrs. B., by the way. She simply had not realized that there was a problem. After we moved to Boston, she often came over to help us make *challos* for Shabbos.

Mrs. B.

Mrs. B. had a hard life. When she reached America from Europe in the late '30s, she discovered that her husband was working in a shoe factory on Shabbos! She was so shocked that she wanted to divorce him and return to Europe at once. When she went to see Rav Pinchas Dovid, however, he talked her out of it. She already had two children and the situation in Europe was becoming quite dangerous. Once the war in Europe broke out, it was clear that he had given her good advice.

Mrs. B. was a great *tzadekes* who *davened* and said *Tehillim* every day. She used to take in *meshulachim,* who paid her for their room and board, so she could give money to *tzedakah.* Unfortunately, life with her husband was extremely difficult, and she also had problems with her two daughters. Her younger daughter did not remain religious and eventually lost contact with her family, and her older daughter never married. She had been offered many *shidduchim,* but didn't agree to any of them. One young man, who had very much wanted to marry her, had a Yiddish accent. One of her "friends" talked her out of the match — and then married him herself!

Mrs. B. passed away on Rav Pinchas Dovid's *yahrtzeit.* Her husband telephoned us in the morning and said that she felt she was going to die. Since it was a Friday, she was afraid that she might not be buried until after Shabbos, and she wanted us to be ready to bury her that very day. An hour and a half later, he called again to say that she had indeed passed away. We all went to her *levayah* that afternoon, as she had asked. Despite her hard life, she was always true to Torah and *mitzvos.*

THIRTEEN

The Rebbe's Family

Reb Shmuel Shmelke

This may be a good place to tell you more about the Rebbe's family. The Rebbe's grandfather, Rav Shmuel Shmelke Horowitz, and his Rebbetzin, Shayna Elka, were both born in Yerushalayim, as were their parents before them. Rebbetzin Shayna was the granddaughter of the Lelover Rebbe, Reb Moshe Biederman, who had come to Yerushalayim from Galicia in 1850. Rav Shmuel Shmelke was the fifth link in the chain leading, son after son, from the famous Rav Shmuel Shmelke Horowitz of Nikolsburg.

Once at a Lag B'Omer *seudah,* I heard the Rebbe tell how his grandfather had received a letter from the Alexanderer Rebbe in Poland. The Alexanderer Rebbe complained that he was so busy advising people that he could not spend enough time learning

The Rebbe's grandmother, Rebbetzin Shayna Elka (Biederman) Horowitz

Torah. He offered Rav Shmuel Shmelke a weekly stipend to support his family of seven or eight children. This would give Reb Shmuel Shmelke more time to learn Torah, and the Alexanderer Rebbe would receive part of the resulting reward in *Olam Haba.*

Reb Shmuel Shmelke wrote back that he would like to help the Alexanderer Rebbe, but that his own life would be too short, a strange prediction for someone in his 30s. However, in 1895, Reb Shmuel Shmelke passed away at the young age of 37. Although his son, Reb Pinchas Dovid, was only 19 at the time, he immediately bought the burial place beside his father on *Har HaZeisim* (the Mount of Olives), where he is buried today. Far from being a bad omen, buying one's burial place is often considered a *segulah* for a long life.

The Kosel

In his letter to the Alexanderer Rebbe, Rav Shmuel Shmelke wrote that the Jews of Yerushalayim had a difficult time on Shabbos when they went to pray at the *Kosel* (Western Wall). At that time, there was only a narrow alleyway in front of the *Kosel;* and the Arabs living in old dilapidated houses there threw eggs and rotten tomatoes at the Jews, ruining their Shabbos clothes. Reb Shmuel Shmelke asked (in vain) the Alexanderer Rebbe to help him purchase those old houses, so they could be demolished to make a large open space in front of the *Kosel* where Jews could pray.

Later, once the buildings became the property of the *Wakf,* the Moslem religious council, this became out of the question. Under the British Mandate, Jews could not even *lein* (read) from the Torah at the *Kosel.* They davened *Shacharis* at the *Kosel* and then had to walk back to their *shuls* in the Old City to *lein.* Then they returned to the *Kosel* for *Mussaf.* The Rebbe still remembers walking to the *Kosel* in 1936 down a narrow street, where Arabs threatened him with the murderous gesture of a finger cutting like a knife across the throat.

In 1967, when we finally got back the Old City, we heard on the radio the sound of Jews *davening Minchah* at the *Kosel.* Then we heard the roar of bulldozers breaking down those old houses to make a wide plaza, just as Reb Shmuel Shmelke had hoped and dreamed!

Rav Pinchas Dovid

Reb Shmuel Shmelke's son was Rav Pinchas Dovid Horowitz, the first Bostoner Rebbe. Sadly, his first Rebbetzin passed away while still very young. Her relatives were very impressed with Rav Pinchas Dovid's *Torah, avodah* and *gemilus chasadim,* and wanted to keep him in the family, so they suggested a match with Soroh Sashe, the daughter of the Turka-Strettiner Rebbe, Rav Yechiel Mechel Brandwein, and a niece of the first Rebbetzin. There was only one problem. The proposed *kallah* was then only six years old!

The Rebbe's father, Rav Pinchas Dovid Horowitz, the first Bostoner Rebbe

Rav Pinchas Dovid also wanted to stay close to their family, so he waited six and a half years for her to become an adult according to *halachah.*

After they were married in 1906, the young couple left Yerushalayim and went up North to live in Tzfas (Safed) near her parents. Three years later, my husband's older brother, the Bostoner Rebbe of New York, Rav Moshe Horowitz, was born. When he was still an infant, his mother took him to bathe in the *Yam HaMelach* (Dead Sea) as a *segulah.*

The Rebbe's great-uncle, the Lelover Rebbe, Rav Dovid'l Biederman, was a great *tzaddik.* He once told the young Rav Pinchas to go to America, but he refused. While on a mission to Galicia in 1913-14, Rav Pinchas Dovid was trapped by the outbreak of World War I. After many adventures he arrived in Greece and escaped on the last neutral ship to leave Athens. It was going to America! After a brief stay in New York, he went to lead a small Chassidic community in Boston.

Meanwhile, World War I brought great poverty and suffering to the Jews of *Eretz Yisrael,* many of whom depended on money from abroad. Rav Pinchas Dovid had disappeared in Poland, and at one point Rebbetzin Soroh Sashe couldn't even afford firewood for heat. After the war she and her son traveled by train through Turkey and Eastern Europe to Turka in Poland, where her father was Rebbe. In 1919 they left to meet Rav Pinchas Dovid in Boston. There she set up an "open house," and soon became well known for her *chessed* and good advice.

A Dream Visit

When Rav Pinchas Dovid came to Boston in 1915, he did not want any publicity; but several incidents made him famous in the local *frum* community. The first involved a prominent family of *shomer Shabbos* Jews who owned a bottling company, a difficult achievement for *frum* Jews in those days. Unfortunately, several members of the family suffered from tuberculosis. One night, the head of the household saw his father in a dream. His father told him, "A *guter Yid* has come to Boston who can give you a *brachah* and advice."

In the dream, the man's father took him by the hand and together they crossed the Cambridge Bridge to the West End of Boston, where Rav Pinchas Dovid lived. The father took his son up to the Rebbe's apartment, showed him the Rebbe and said, "This is the man whom I want you to visit."

Then the dream ended and the man woke up. The next morning, the man took his nephew and together they crossed the Cambridge Bridge to the West End. Eventually they found the very same apartment he had seen in his dream. The man knocked and entered but, when he actually saw Rav Pinchas Dovid in the flesh, he fainted!

Rav Pinchas Dovid did advise him about many matters. The man and his family members were cured of their tuberculosis, *Baruch Hashem,* and their business prospered. Their children, grandchildren and great-grandchildren still come to my husband for advice.

Rebbetzin Gittel

Rebbetzin Soroh Sashe used to tell a miraculous story about her mother, Rebbetzin Gittel Brandwein. Her family lived in Tiveria (Tiberias) on the shore of Lake Kinneret. Later she moved to Tzfas. During the earthquake of 1837, Rebbetzin Gittel's house collapsed and she was buried under the rubble. When she opened her eyes, she saw a vision of her dead grandfather and grandmother standing in front of her, holding up a heavy roof beam so it wouldn't fall on her. Eventually, some townspeople came by calling out, "Anybody alive in there?" She answered, and they dug her out and saved her life.

Rebbetzin Soroh Sashe

The Rebbe's mother, Rebbetzin Soroh Sashe, was named after the mother of Reb Levi Yitzchak of Berditchev, and she was his sixth-generation descendant. We lived together in Boston where, even in her old age, she remained a wonderful *balabusta* who loved cooking, loved people and knew exactly how a *Rabbanishe* house should be run. She used to spend hours telling *Chassidishe* stories to our children and had a great influence on them.

She also taught them by example. She taught them with the look of *yiras Shamayim* on her face on *Erev Yom Kippur* when, all dressed in white, she lit her *gezunt licht* and *neshamah licht*, and prayed that our family should be *zocheh* to a good year. She taught them by saying *Tehillim* and *davening* out loud with intense concentration. Both she and my own mother used to read the Yiddish *Tz'enah U'renah* commentary on the *sedrah* each week. Some weeks, when the *sedrah* was a particularly long one, it took them until Tuesday; but they always finished it. Seeing such things daily taught our children more than all the sermons in the world.

The Rebbe

My husband, the present Bostoner Rebbe שליט"א, was born in Boston in 1921. We had many similar experiences as children. We both lived outside of New York, had few religious friends and were often lonely. I, at least, went to school; but the Rebbe stayed at home all day, learning with his brother or old European tutors (who sometimes fell asleep during lessons). One bright spot was Mr. Edward Gerber, a religious Boston lawyer, and later a brother-in-law of Rav Yosef Ber Soloveitchik. He used to teach the Rebbe reading, writing and arithmetic. Other than that, the Rebbe grew up mostly with *meshulachim,* rather than friends his own age.

In 1934, the year my husband became *bar mitzvah,* the entire family moved back to *Eretz Yisrael,* and the Rebbe went to his first *yeshivah,* Torah V'Yirah in Meah Shearim. This was his first chance to learn intensively with other young men, and he loved every minute of it. When his family had to move back to America two years later, for financial reasons, the Rebbe wanted to go to *yeshivah* there too. His father felt that there weren't any real *yeshivos* in America; but Mr. Gerber told him about Yeshivah Torah Vodaath, which Rav Shraga Feivel Mendlowitz had started in New York. There the Rebbe went to the *mesivta's bais medrash* (the top class of the *yeshivah*); and there he received his *semichah* (Rabbinic ordination) from Rav Shlomo Heiman, *the Rosh HaYeshivah.*

The Rebbe was popular among his classmates, even though he was one of the few *Chassidishe bachurim* in the *yeshivah*. Even then he had a knack for leadership and a lovely sense of humor. Rav Mendlowitz himself once predicted that his shy *Chassidishe* student would become a great Rebbe.

The Niggun

In 1935, when the Rebbe was still in Jerusalem, the Modzhitzer Rebbe came from Europe for a visit. There he introduced his unique melodies, which were unlike anything the Jewish world was used to. Most familiar *niggunim* resembled simple East European folk songs, marches and waltzes, with lots of choruses. The Modzhitzer *niggunim* were long and complex compositions, with few repeats, and lots of sudden unexpected changes in direction. They were an instant sensation and people all over town kept repeating them and trying to piece them together. The Rebbe learned several, and was one of the first to bring them to America a year later.

Two years later the Rebbe started learning at Mesivta Torah Vodaath. One Shabbos at *Shalosh Seudos,* Rav Mendlowitz asked the Rebbe to lead "Yedid Nefesh," usually a typical calm, if not sleepy, melody. Instead, the Rebbe launched into a Modzhitzer version that began with a crashing "Bim bom!" The *bachurim* were stunned; but Rav Mendlowitz, who had an ear for a good *niggun,* had the Rebbe repeat it week after week until they all learned it. Even at summer camp, whenever they met the Rebbe, other Torah Vodaath *bachurim* would greet him with a good-natured "Bim bom!" Once the Rebbe's father moved to Williamsburg, New York, in 1939, the Rebbe was able to introduce many of his friends to *Chassidus* through his father.

Mr. Singer

Another "almost member-of-the-family" was Mr. Singer. He was sort of a *shamash* for the Rebbe and his father for over 50 years. He was an eccentric old bachelor who was quite educated. He was brought up by an aristocratic Jewish family in Russia, and he used to play music for wealthy Russian aristocrats at concerts and dances. In the United States, he once gave a violin concert with the sister of Jascha Heifetz. I understand that she had been interested in marrying Mr. Singer, but that he had discouraged her.

After accumulating a comfortable fortune as a concert violinist, Mr. Singer took his savings and bought a sightseeing boat, which ferried people back and forth across the Charles River in Boston. He hired a man to act as his manager and run the boat. Unfortunately, the manager once tried to throw in the heavy anchor all by himself. He fell in with it and drowned. When the police came to question Mr. Singer about the case, he thought that they were going to arrest him. The shock and worry precipitated a nervous breakdown.

Mr. Singer's mother, who was very religious, had become old and frail, and she knew that she could not live much longer. When she saw that her son was unable to take care of himself, she took him to see Rav Pinchas Dovid, the first Bostoner Rebbe, and told him that her son would be glad to help out in the house in any way needed. This worked out fine and eventually Mr. Singer moved in. In fact, he did a bit of everything: shopping, fixing, cleaning, odd jobs, errands. He even used to take the Rebbe and his sister (and later our own children) out for their daily rides in their carriages.

Mr. Singer particularly liked wearing his blue "Boston Special Police" uniform during these outings. He got the uniform by registering as a "guard" for the Rebbe's father and the *shul*. Although

Mr. Singer wasn't really the policeman type — he was actually quite nervous and meek — he dearly loved his uniform.

Mr. Singer Visits

The Shabbos that I was engaged, my mother went to visit Rebbetzin Soroh Sashe around *Shalosh Seudos* time, and I was alone at home. All of a sudden, there was a knock at the door. When I asked who was there, a man answered, "I want to meet the *kallah*!" It was Mr. Singer!

Mother and I had just arrived in New York from Los Angeles, and we didn't have all those things a *balabusta* can pull out of the refrigerator or pantry at a moment's notice for sudden visitors. I felt very embarrassed because we had no refreshments left in the house; all our Shabbos fruits and cakes had already been served to other guests earlier in the afternoon. I sat down to a simple *Shalosh Seudos* meal of matzah and sardines, and I couldn't offer Mr. Singer anything except soda. After that, he always teased me about how poor and frugal we must have been to have had nothing to offer him besides soda.

I later found out that Mr. Singer told the Rebbe that he was against our *shidduch* "on principle." He himself had remained a bachelor, and he felt that the Rebbe didn't have to get married either! Later, when Mr. Singer visited us in Boston, he did approve of me. He even gave me money to go to a fine department store to buy a beautiful new dress as his wedding gift.

I once asked Mr. Singer why he had never married. After all, his father had married. "Ah, that was different," he said, "My father married my mother, but why should I take in some stranger and support her?"

FOURTEEN

The Early Years

Getting Ready

During the year of our engagement, the Rebbe was on the East Coast learning at Yeshivah Torah Vodaath, while I spent much of my time on the West Coast, getting ready for our wedding. One of our good friends in Los Angeles had a married daughter, and I asked if I could use her wedding gown. It was a little tight, so I had it altered to fit me; and I also had a new veil made. The color of the dress was off-white, because my family custom is not to wear white wedding gowns.

Our Wedding

The Rebbe's father was one of the first major *Chassidishe* Rebbes in Williamsburg, and had been "adopted" by many people whose own *Rebbeim* were far away in Europe. That meant that literally thousands of people wanted to attend our wedding. It was one of the first large *Chassidishe* weddings in New York but, for Mother's sake, I tried to cut corners when making wedding plans. She was widowed and already burdened with so many debts.

We had always enjoyed sharing things with others, and ours was a very big, very beautiful, *Chassidishe* wedding. It was held in two halls in Empire Manor in Brooklyn. The women used the downstairs hall; and the men, the upstairs one, coming downstairs only for the *mitzvah tantz.* Three thousand people attended the *chuppah;* and 900 invited guests came to the meal. I was seated on a platform, as is the custom, and two adorable twin girls came up to sit with me. They were Rebbetzin Soroh Sashe's younger sisters. Today these two little girls are the Skverer Rebbetzin of Borough Park and Rebbetzin Shprintze Landau of Veretzky.

In those days, *glatt kosher* catering did not exist. For the wedding, we had to get 1,000 new china plates and 1,000 new soup bowls, and to *kasher* 1,000 settings of silverware. That in itself was a huge task. This was 50 years ago, and we still have some of those plates. Everything was organized by Rebbetzin Soroh Sashe and my brother-in-law, the Bostoner Rebbe of New York, since Mother and I had gone back to California; but both families shared the expenses.

Our First Home

At the time of our marriage, the Rebbe was still learning full-time in *yeshivah,* and my mother had agreed to support us with $40 a month, a huge sum in those days. She was also supposed to give us the Williamsburg apartment to live in. Since I knew that she did not have that much money, I suggested that she rent out the Williamsburg apartment instead. That way she got $35 a month in rent and only had to add another $5 each month.

Meanwhile, the Rebbe and I moved into a room on the top floor of Rebbetzin Soroh Sashe's house. My brother-in-law, Rav Moshe

Horowitz, was now the Bostoner Rebbe of New York, and he had a *shul* and a *mikveh* on the ground floor. Rebbetzin Soroh Sashe lived on the second floor, where there was a bedroom, dining room, waiting room, living room and a small guest room. The third floor was rented. My brother-in-law, his family and his sister lived on the fourth floor. The fifth floor had several bedrooms. Some were for Mr. Singer and the *meshulachim;* and one became ours.

When we finally came home from our wedding — at about 4 a.m. — I heard an alarm clock go off in the next room. The Rebbe explained that Mr. Singer always got up at 4 a.m! When I asked him why, Mr. Singer would only say that he liked to get the percolated coffee ready and to clean up the kitchen. Years later he told me that, in Russia, his father used to get up early to feed their chickens, ducks and geese. I told him, "Here we don't have any ducks or geese to feed. Why not sleep a bit later?" but it was no use. I guess it was just habit.

Mother

After my wedding Mother went back to the West Coast for a year. She sold our house in Los Angeles and used some of the money to fix the heating system in the Williamsburg house. She set the rest aside for my sister's wedding and *naddan.* Then she moved back to Williamsburg so Chaya Yehudis, who had just turned 12, could go to the Bais Yaakov High School. They lived together until my sister got married to a nephew of the Clevelander Rebbe, Rav Usher Mordechai Rosenbaum, the Stroznitzer-Clevelander Rebbe.

Mother established the first major Hachnasas Kallah Fund in Williamsburg, and was always holding parlor-meetings for one good cause or another. At Mother's *levayah,* the Satmar Rebbetzin said that she had learned how to raise money for *tzedakah* from my mother. Mother developed congestive heart failure in the 1960s and, during her last years, Chaya Yehudis' daughter, Leah Bina, stayed with her to take care of her.

In 1976, Mother had to go to the hospital for a particularly serious operation. She told Leah Bina, "If I don't come back from the hospital, I want you to know that in my drawer you will find an envelope with $150 in it. During my *shivah,* someone will come and ask for it. You must tell him, 'I am sorry, but you will have to come back after the *shivah* is over.' That is what I want you to do."

A few months later my mother, Rochma Miril Leifer, the Clevelander Rebbetzin, passed away. During the *shivah* a man came, just as she had predicted, and claimed the envelope. They told him to come back after the week of *shivah* was over, and he did. My mother wanted to do *chessed* for everybody, even after her death.

Dainty Edges

In 1942, however, the burning issue was how the newly ordained Rabbi Levi Yitzchak Horowitz was going to support his young family, especially since, although he could have been a Rebbe in several places, he did not want to enter the Rabbinate. He was afraid it would take too much time away from his learning.

Next to our room was a "souvenir" of his first attempt to avoid the Rabbinate, a diamond-polishing wheel. The Rebbe had once hoped to earn a part-time living polishing diamonds, something he could do at home after a full day of learning in *yeshivah.* Unfortunately, he was not very successful at it. He told me that he spent more time searching for dropped diamonds than he did polishing them! By the time we were married, he had rented the wheel out to other *yeshivah bachurim.* I remember that it made a horrible grinding noise late into the night.

A few months after we were married, a man from Connecticut came to visit. He was looking for an investor to back his new stationery business, "Dainty Edges," and he had heard that we had a dowry of ready cash. From the beginning, I was not interested in his proposal. I felt that we should buy furniture with the money, so we could eventually furnish our own apartment. On the other hand, if the stationery business prospered, we would have a guaranteed income that would allow the Rebbe to remain in *yeshivah* full-time. The stationery man took a thousand dollars from us and, not long afterwards, came back to ask for a second thousand. Unfortunately, the business did not do well.

In a way, thousands of people all over the world benefited from the failure of "Dainty Edges." It was a *chessed* in disguise, because it convinced my husband that Hashem wanted him to become a Rebbe.

Our First Son, Reb Pinchas

Later that year, I was expecting our first child. Things were rough, mainly because all my other work and responsibilities did not just disappear. The doctors told me that the baby would be born just before Pesach; but I prayed that he would be born after Pesach. I had so much work to do! As it turned out, my prayer was answered.

With each of my children, I first had a dream telling me after whom to name the child. Early in my first pregnancy, I dreamt that my father-in-law, Rav Pinchas Dovid, was being brought to Israel in a metal coffin to be buried on *Har HaZeisim* in Jerusalem. Rav Pinchas Dovid had indeed wanted to be buried on *Har HaZeisim* next to his father but, when he passed away in 1941, the war made this impossible. It was still impossible at the time of my dream; but later, in 1946, the Rebbe was able to take his father's remains back to Israel on the first Israel-bound freighter to leave the United States after the war. Because of health regulations, the original coffin, still unopened, was placed inside a metal one, just as in my dream. He was eventually buried on *Har HaZeisim* without any coffin at all, as is the custom in Jerusalem. The Rabbis who reinterred him were amazed that his body, despite years underground, a lengthy sea voyage and a jolting truck trip from Haifa, was still intact. It showed what a great *tzaddik* he was.

I felt that the dream was very significant and, when my husband later asked if I would mind naming our first child Pinchas Dovid, I agreed right away. He was surprised, since the custom is usually for the mother to choose the first name, and to honor someone in her own family. I explained my reason to him and, later, to my mother. In fact, Pinchas resembles his *zeide* and namesake very much.

Pinchas, while a joy, was an early bird who got up around 4:30 or 5:00 every morning! This was fine on Friday, when there was so much to do for Shabbos; but during the week I would have enjoyed sleeping a little later. As a first-time mother, I was happy, if exhausted; but even greater challenges lay ahead.

Return to Boston

The Rebbe's father had always wanted his eldest son, Rav Moshe, to take over his *Rabbanus* in New York, and his youngest son, Rav Levi Yitzchak, to return and strengthen what was left of the Bostoner Community in Boston. And so it was. Rav Moshe Horowitz became the Bostoner Rebbe of New York after his father's passing in 1941, and we left for Boston in 1944.

We went back that first summer totally alone. Anyone seeing us get off the train at South Station certainly wouldn't have thought that we were going to make much of a difference to Boston, or anywhere else for that matter. We were just another young couple in our early 20s, coming with suitcases and dreams. But the Rebbe had vision and determination, and Hashem was very good to us.

In Boston, we first stayed at the old Peabody House on Poplar Street, which had been the Chassidic Center of the Rebbe's father in the West End. It had once been a mansion, and then a social center for foreigners and children. Now it was old and dilapidated, and certainly no place for a young nursing mother with her first child. It had broken windows, round-bellied ceilings and a whole zooful of insects. I remember watching those insects every time I nursed my son. I was fascinated by how they could fly back and forth so quickly without collisions or a traffic cop!

Our apartment had an old-fashioned kitchen, including two tables — one *milchig,* one *fleishig* — with bottom shelves for pots and pans. There were no cupboards, only those extra boards under each table. The West End was no longer a Jewish neighborhood, so we had to "import" friends and *meshulachim* to make a *minyan* for Shabbos.

Rough Times

I soon discovered that taking care of a first baby can be quite difficult for a new mother with no family around to help her. It wasn't that I didn't know how to take care of babies; after all, I had helped take care of my younger sister, Chaya Yehudis. I just wasn't used to handling so many things at once all by myself — doing the housework and taking care of guests, while nursing, feeding and diapering a new, and rather colicky, baby. It wasn't easy, especially preparing for Shabbos on my own, but I managed somehow. At least I was used to being busy!

Meanwhile, the Rebbe was having it no easier. There were almost no *Chassidim* left in Boston from the early days. The few members of the Rebbe's father's congregation that were left were now over 70! Worse, many of them were non-observant, since most *frum* members had either passed away or left for New York. It must have been the congregation with the oldest congregants, outside an old-age home, anywhere in the country! The local *mikveh* was questionable, there was no *cholov Yisrael* milk or *glatt kosher* meat, the hospitals didn't let frum *mohelim* perform *brissim* and didn't offer kosher food, there was no *shomer Shabbos* bakery, and so on. What was a 23-year-old "Grand Rabbi" and communal leader supposed to do?

If anyone had told me then, as I sat watching the bugs climb the Peabody House curtains, that 50 years later Boston would have all those things and more, and that we would have one of the youngest congregations in the country, I am not sure what I would have thought. I certainly wouldn't have pictured my dining room in Har Nof full of young men from M.I.T., Harvard and Brandeis dressed in *bekeshes* and *shtriemlach*!

Dorchester

We soon moved out of the West End to Dorchester, then an up-and-coming Jewish neighborhood. A small group of Bostoner *Chassidim* had bought an old dilapidated house there in the hopes that the Rebbe's father, or one of his sons, would come back. The Rebbe's father had even visited the house once, but it stayed empty and unrenovated for years. It was little more than an empty shell, called by the locals, appropriately enough, "the haunted house." It had no electrical fixtures, the windows were broken and boarded up, and even the floor had been torn up to make room for the plumbing. We had to start from scratch to make it into a livable house and *shul.*

On the other hand, our Dorchester house, haunted or not, was quite spacious. The first floor eventually had a *shul* on one side, and the Rebbe's office, our kitchen and our dining room on the

Once it was fixed up, our "haunted house" at 61 Columbia Road, Dorchester, was our home, and that of the New England Chassidic Center for 18 years

other. The second floor had five bedrooms, and the gabled attic had another two. The large basement housed our *mikveh,* boiler, Pesach kitchen and — during the freezing Boston winters — our clotheslines.

By Rosh Hashanah renovations were far enough along for us to be able to *daven* in the *shul,* although we had to live a few blocks away. We moved in a few weeks later, although we still had no central heat. We tried using small kerosene heaters; but we hadn't reckoned on Boston's harsh winters. Soon the snow was almost man-high and the house was not warm enough for our seven-month-old baby, who got sick with pneumonia. I also came down with a bad cold, and the baby and I had to go back to New York. We returned to Boston in February, when there were finally working radiators in most of the rooms.

Of course, February in Boston is the coldest month of all. On the afternoon that the Rebbe and I came back from New York, a terrible blizzard was blowing outside. The wind was howling, and tree branches were banging against our new glass windows. I was just straightening things out and getting ready to cook supper when, all of a sudden, our doorbell began ringing again and again. Then the baby began crying for his bottle. While trying to take care of him, I ran down the steps to see who was at the door.

The Boarder

At first, I saw only a sort of shadow. Finally I made out the shape of a small woman wearing a heavy shawl. I opened the door and she said in Yiddish, *"Men ken nisht aroislazen a hint in dem veter* — Let me in! You can't let a dog stay outside in such weather. I am a good Jewish daughter, and I heard that you have rooms to rent."

"You can come inside," I told her, "but I'm sorry, we don't rent out rooms. We have no electricity on the third floor, and all the bedrooms on the lower floors are taken up by our family, so I simply don't have a place where you can stay. The attic room has heat, but no electricity."

She said, "Show me the attic room and I will see if it is good." Not wanting to argue, I took her upstairs. She felt the bed to see if the mattress was soft enough and felt the radiators to see if there was enough steam heat. Since there was no electricity upstairs, and thus no lights, I took her up there with a candle and told her to put out the candle when she came back down, so she would not accidentally start a fire. Meanwhile, I had to go downstairs to take care of the baby.

Later, our new "guest" came down and asked me if we needed a woman to cook for us. I told her that we could cook for ourselves. She began fuming, "Don't think just because you are a Rebbetzin, you are going to boss me around!" I told her, "I didn't even hire you, so how can I boss you around!" It was all too clear by then that she was mentally ill.

I served our "guest" supper in the kitchen once the baby went to sleep. The blizzard was so intense that, although the kitchen doorway was covered with two blankets to keep out the draft, it was still quite cold. When I asked the old lady if she had put out the candle in her room, she started fuming again, "No, and if you don't like it, you can put it out yourself!" I was afraid the candle might start a fire, so I walked all the way back up to the attic and put it out myself.

Having survived supper, I now tried to get everyone to bed. Unfortunately, we had only one working bathroom in the house, on the middle floor. That night, our mysterious guest went in, locked the door, took a long bath, washed her dress and stockings, and hung everything out to dry. She stayed in there for two hours! Although exhausted from the trip, I couldn't get to bed until midnight.

The next morning was the calm after the storm. It was a bright, beautiful day, and everything was covered with a blanket of shining white snow. People managed to get out and the carpenters soon arrived to fix our *shul* doors. In America the doors of public buildings must open towards the outside to prevent people from being trapped inside in case of a fire. Our "guest" soon began quarreling with the carpenters, insisting that the doors open the other way, until I had to tell her, "Leave them alone. It's the law!"

I gave her breakfast, then lunch, and finally five dollars. I told her where she could rent a room, and explained that she could not stay with us, because we had men guests coming (quite true). In those days, you could easily rent a room for five dollars. She answered, "I'm sorry, but I like your cooking, and I'm not leaving!" I said, "I would love to have you, but I don't have room. I want you to go by yourself; but if you don't, I'll call the police. We simply have no room for you here." Once again, Reb Yankele's method worked like a charm. "O.K.," she said, taking the five dollars, "I'll leave."

I later found out that this woman used to live with her cousin, who had sent her out on that cold stormy night. Her cousin didn't want her there anymore, so she simply told her that we rented out rooms! I thought it was terrible for someone — especially a relative — to send an old woman outdoors on such a miserable night. Still, these elderly people with emotional problems can be quite difficult.

The Community

Meanwhile, the Rebbe refused to be discouraged by his elderly, largely "under-observant" congregation. He took his small flock in hand, and plunged right into making them *baalei teshuvah.* Thus, although the Rebbe is now best known for his hundreds of college-age *baalei teshuvah,* his first "successes" were people in their 70s and 80s! It was quite an experience. One old man told the Rebbe that he hadn't put on *tefillin* for 65 years. The Rebbe helped him start again, but the first time his elderly protege put on his *tefillin shel rosh,* they fell down onto his nose. "*Oy*!" he said, "*Der kopf is eingeshrinken* — My head must have shrunk!"

Another *baal teshuvah,* age 78, used to come to *shul* at 3 a.m. every morning to learn and to cry by himself. He had his own key to let himself into the *shul.* His wife was 84 years old; and he was her fourth husband. When he passed away, his wife refused to renew her front-row seat for Rosh Hashanah. She was sure she was going to die. We begged her not to give up her seat, but she insisted that she was going to the hospital and would die there. Rebbetzin Soroh Sashe told her, *"Men lebt nisht tzu order un men shtarbt nish tzu order* — You don't live to order and you don't die to order!" but it was no use.

Mrs. R. did go to the hospital but, despite all her dire predictions, she came back alive and well in time for Rosh Hashanah. She wanted her old seat back, but it had already been sold to someone else. The only way out of this dilemma was for me to give her my seat and to go sit in the back of the women's section. Later, she moved into an old-age home and lived to be 99. I often visited her there.

Another part of our first Boston community were refugees from Europe. The Rebbe often advised them to move to New York where their children could have a better Torah education. I remember telling him once, "You're sending away all the good *baalabatim,*" but the Rebbe answered, "I can't advise them what's good for me. I have to advise them what's good for them!"

Quietly and slowly, our community seemed to be dying out. Even my children's pediatrician asked me what my children would do when they grew up. They all wanted to be teachers and Chassidic Rebbes, but who would be left to teach? He said, "Jews today are more or less secular. What's going to be?" Later he realized that there is a future for *frum Yiddishkeit.* In fact, today, Boston's Jewish community is known for its college-educated religious young people.

Even now, Boston is a largely transient community. Every year, over 130,000 students arrive to attend college, leaving after graduation if they can't land a job in the area. Many of them keep in touch with us, even after they leave the neighborhood, and we meet them years later all over the world, in England, Switzerland, Israel and Australia.

Steady Progress

In those days, Boston still had several elderly Orthodox Rabbis who had been trained in the great *yeshivos* of Europe. Although great scholars, they spoke mostly Yiddish, and felt that their European accents and lack of American "culture" prevented them from influencing the wider community. They came to the Rebbe, who was American born and spoke excellent English, and they asked him to become more involved in community affairs and to be their spokesman. At first the Rebbe, who was then still in his 20s and 30s, felt embarrassed to be speaking for such distinguished Rabbis; but they kept begging him to speak for them and, *Baruch Hashem,* he began to see great success in his efforts. At first it was fundraising for *shuls,* schools and *mikvaos.* Then he began to tackle more controversial community-wide problems.

For example, the Rebbe went to the new Beth Israel Hospital maternity ward and convinced them to allow properly trained *mohelim* to perform *brissim.* This was particularly important because, in those days, new mothers stayed in the hospital far longer than eight days. The Rebbe also arranged for *mikvaos* in Boston's funeral chapels, and *glatt kosher* meat and *cholov Yisrael* milk deliveries from New York. Evidently, he even convinced a local bakery to close its doors on Shabbos. Now in Boston you can get all kinds of kosher food. There are four *shomer Shabbos* bakeries, two kosher-only grocery stores, *milchig, fleishig* and *parve* restaurants, and even a kosher pizza parlor.

FIFTEEN

At Home

Bless the Inventors

Life in Dorchester was soon busier than ever. Being a Rebbetzin doesn't mean just sitting in a chair and saying nice things to people. It's a lot of work, especially when your home is always open for community affairs and 10 to 15 guests sleep over at a time. It was especially hard in the early years, when we couldn't afford much help.

My day began when our baby woke up between 4:30-5:00 in the morning. Getting dressed, getting breakfast for us and a dozen guests, who came in at odd hours, taking care of the baby — this was just the start. My "housework" included washing the floors of the *shul* downstairs and making all 13 beds. Changing 13 beds every week required a tremendous amount of linen. The sheets were sent to a laundry service, but I used to stay up until 2 a.m. many evenings washing towels, pillowcases and all our clothes on a metal scrubboard. We didn't get a washing machine until I had Shayna, our third child.

Then there was the food. Since everything had to be absolutely kosher, we had to make almost everything ourselves — not just bread, but also butter, cheese and even noodles — for us and all our guests. We were cooking all week.

As for cheese, the only kind I could make was cottage cheese. First I let the milk sour; then I drained it in a cheesecloth to get the curds. It didn't smell anything like the containers of cottage cheese you buy in the store today. On the other hand, in the summertime, I made delicious homemade ice cream and blueberry pie. Such kosher treats were not available in any store, so you made them yourself or did without.

I remember when we got our first freezer; it was a real blessing, a dream come true. Now I could cook and bake ahead of time. Mrs. Pauline Schiffman, a very dear friend of mine, gave it to me; and I blessed her every time I used it — for almost 20 years. I also remember my first washing machine. Before that, my arms used to ache from scrubbing all the laundry. I want to give a special *brachah* to all those inventors who have helped hardworking Jewish housewives!

Rebbetzin Soroh Sashe

We lived together with the Rebbe's mother, Rebbetzin Soroh Sashe. She knew a great deal about running a *Rebbeishe* household but she couldn't help very much because she was ill with high blood pressure. Remembering my years with my stepfather, I advised her to stay away from caffeine and salt; but that was difficult for her. She had grown up in *Eretz Yisrael,* where she used to drink five to six cups of coffee a day and eat very spicy and salty food. Many years later the Rebbe's brother, the Bostoner Rebbe of New York, had a heart attack and visited the famous cardiologist, Dr. Paul Dudley White, in Boston. Dr. White told him to avoid caffeine and salt in order to lower his blood pressure, and then Rebbetzin Soroh Sashe finally agreed to do the same.

Later, we made quite a pair. She had trouble with her gall bladder, and I had trouble with my ulcer, so I used to cook the same meals for both of us, because neither could eat salty or spicy foods.

The Rebbe's mother, Rebbetzin Soroh Sashe (left), came to live with us in Boston

When Rebbetzin Soroh Sashe's high blood pressure became more severe, I spoke to Dr. Dubins, her physician. I asked if resting in bed all the time was really good for her. I felt, and he agreed, that she needed to be out of bed for several hours each day. I knew she wouldn't be happy just sitting or doing "busy work," so we tried to include her in the life of the family. I arranged things so that she could help in the kitchen.

I would cook the noodles and prepare the eggs, oil and spices; then she would mix them together to make the *lokshen kugel* for Shabbos. Mr. Singer would peel the potatoes, he and I would grate them and then she would make the *potato kugel.* I would make and knead the *challah* dough on Friday — 25 pounds at a time — and then Rebbetzin Soroh Sashe would braid the *challos.* She was a very talented braider, and could make *challos* for Shabbos, ladder and bird *challos* for *Erev Yom Kippur,* and hand-shaped *challos* for *Hoshana Rabbah.* We made sure she was included, and it was good for all of us.

I learned from her how to measure with my eye and hand. My own mother was very precise and always measured everything just so. I find it much easier and faster to simply throw the ingredients in, and the dish almost always turns out the same. When I bake a cake, however, I do measure out the exact quantities with a measuring cup, because otherwise the cake doesn't come out right.

Mr. Singer in Boston

The last permanent member of our household was Mr. Singer, who came from New York during our second spring in Boston. He was an enthusiastic helper and a good friend through the years, although he certainly had his eccentricities. For example, he got himself appointed as a Boston Special Police Officer to the Chassidic Center and, thereafter, would never be seen without his dark blue uniform. He would lug vegetables home from the grocery store and wheel the Rebbe's carriage to the park while wearing his uniform. To this day people still tell the Rebbe about the policeman who wheeled him to the park. Many years later, Mr. Singer took Reb Pinchas and our other children out for rides in their carriages. That was a big help, since it let me do my work in peace.

Mr. Singer's first job each day was rather unusual. We only used *cholov Yisrael* milk, which is watched from the time of milking by a trustworthy Jew. In those days there was no commercial *cholov Yisrael* milk in Boston and Mr. Singer used to get up at dawn and take a bus all the way to Chelsea, which still had farms in those days. He would watch the cows being milked, and then carry our milk home in big metal jugs in time for breakfast.

Mr. Singer could not stand all our guests and our "open door" policy, and he was always threatening to leave. For example, one year, we arranged a big Lag B'Omer celebration. In *Eretz Yisrael* the *Chassidim* sing "Bar Yochai" and dance around huge bonfires. Because of Boston's fire laws, we had to settle for a "mini-bonfire" in a large pan. Our *Chassidim* sang and danced around it with gusto and, afterwards, we had a large crowd of guests join us for a big *seudah.* Since we had no plastic or paper plates, and had to wash everything by hand, the work was overwhelming. In the middle of all this, Mr. Singer came in and told me that he couldn't take it anymore. He was leaving! I looked him straight in the eye and told him, "It's your choice, but who is going to take care of you when you are sick?" Fortunately that did it!

Actually his illnesses were no joking matter. A few weeks before, he had had an ear infection that interfered with his sense of balance, and the Rebbe and I had to stay up nights with him. Rebbetzin Soroh Sashe told me that the Rebbe's father had actually tried to get Mr. Singer to leave. He used to tell him: "It isn't right for a man to be alone. Go out and get married!" In practice, however, Mr. Singer left only once, and soon came back again. He just couldn't seem to find a suitable place for himself.

More Meshulachim

Then there were the *meshulachim,* our ever-present, unannounced, long-term, free-of-charge houseguests. In fact, sometimes they seemed more like the hosts! Every morning the *meshulachim davened* and then ate breakfast, usually about 8:30 or 9:00 a.m. That meant that I could never get an early start on my day, because I could not leave the house until I had made them breakfast and helped them get to where they needed to go.

In those days, *meshulachim* did not have drivers to take them to the homes of potential donors. They had to travel by trolley, tram or foot. Besides making their beds and feeding them three meals a day, I also had to write out the names and addresses of all the local shuls and *baalabatim* for them. Today, such a list could be photocopied, but then it had to be handwritten, time after time, for each *meshulach.* Later, I asked the Rebbe to hire a secretary to maintain a file of *shul* addresses, to send out reminders for *shul* meetings, to answer telephone calls and to handle some of the *meshulach* list-making.

Many *meshulachim* expected us to give them a car to drive to their meetings. They could not believe that the Bostoner Rebbe did not have a car! The only access we had to a car was through a good friend of ours, whose husband would sometimes drive us places.

When *meshulachim* would ask me, "Well, if you have to go to an affair, what do you do?" I told them the truth, "I call a taxi."

Rabbi Reines

Some *meshulachim* were quite charitable themselves. I remember, for example, Rabbi Reines, who used to arrive lugging a huge suitcase. He would set it down in the hall with a loud thump and announce in a cheerful voice "It's Rabbi Reines, with the *tienes* (complaints)!" Actually, his suitcase was not loaded with complaints, or much of anything else. I once asked him why he needed it. He said, "When people see me coming with such a large suitcase, they get worried that I am going to stay a long time. That way they are glad to give me a quick donation and get rid of me!"

When he first came to Boston in the 1940s, we were trying to raise money for a diabetic *shochet* who was in the hospital. When Rabbi Reines heard about it, he offered to help us; he wanted "to be part of the *mitzvah.*" He told us to call Chicago, and to tell his banking agent that he wanted to contribute $150! Since he was obviously well off — $150 was a lot of money in those days — I asked him what he did with the money he collected. He gave it all away to charity. He was divorced and was tired of just sitting at home alone; so he decided to go out and do *mitzvos* for others in this personal way.

The Bostoner Hotel and Infirmary

My hardest job was taking care of the *meshulachim* when they became ill. Once, when our third son, Rav Naftali, was a small boy, he came down with pneumonia. I hardly had time to take care of him, because a *meshulach* living with us was also sick, and I was busy all day taking the *meshulach's* temperature, carrying his meals to his upstairs bedroom and calling his doctor. I finally asked this *meshulach* why he didn't go back to his own home in Williamsburg, and have his own wife take care of him. He seemed surprised by the question. His wife had to take care of their small children. It would be far too hard for her to take care of him as well!

Another time, when I was expecting, we had family guests staying with us. I was so busy serving breakfast to our children, our guests and the *meshulachim* that, before I looked around, it was 1 p.m. Lunchtime already! So, without a break, I prepared sardine sandwiches for the family, so everyone could go to the park and spend the day boating on the Boston Commons. I was just about to have a sandwich myself, when a *meshulach* came in for lunch. I gave him a sardine sandwich but, when he saw butter in it, he refused to eat it. I explained that I was brought up in a *Rebbeishe* house and that butter (but not milk) may be used with fish. The *meshulach* said that he did not use any dairy products at all with fish, and so I had to leave my own sandwich sitting on the table while I cooked a full *fleishig* meal for him.

Unfortunately, I often forgot my *zeide's* advice to my mother when she was a little girl. Exhausting yourself with one *chessed* can keep you from doing another. In this particular case, the strain took its toll. I soon became quite sick myself and could not take care of anyone for quite some time. I also developed an ulcer, perhaps because I did not have enough time to eat or sleep properly. My days were very long, and tiring. Still, I was happy. We were helping others and making a difference.

On Chessed and Sacrifice

The long hours and constant work even had their humorous side. There were times, on *Erev Shabbos,* when I literally did not have time to wash my face and hands. I just had to get dressed for Shabbos as I was!

Is such a life reasonable? I have my own way of looking at it. Once you decide you want to spend your life doing things for other people, you have to accept the bad with the good. In the old days, there certainly was not much glamor or thanks, and a lot of drudgery and hard work. Even in those days, the average Rebbetzin probably did not put up with an open house like ours. A guest once told me that he had never seen people tolerate so much; but this was part of our *avodah,* our service.

Mr. Singer Versus the Meshulachim

People differ, and Mr. Singer could not stand all the *meshulachim.* My mother-in-law and I would feed them all throughout the day and the kitchen would get messy with a lot of dishes. That meant a lot more work for Mr. Singer. Furthermore, the *meshulachim* were pretty gruff with him. Still, I can't blame them entirely, because Mr. Singer was pretty gruff with them too.

One night, when we lived on Columbia Road, Mr. Singer secretly locked the kitchen door, so the *meshulachim* could not go in for a cup of coffee during the night. Later, Mr. Singer himself came down, forgot he had locked the door and banged his nose on it! When he began to yell at the *meshulachim,* I told him, "It's your own fault. You locked the door," but he was not consoled. Another time, Mr. Singer left out spoiled milk for the *meshulachim* to use in their morning coffee. The Rebbe came down, made himself a cup of coffee, poured in some of the milk, and found himself another one of Mr. Singer's victims!

There was one *meshulach* that Mr. Singer especially disliked. One night Mr. Singer put out the hall light to make it difficult for this *meshulach* to see his way downstairs. Sure enough, that very same night, Mr. Singer slipped in the dark and hurt himself. I told him, *"Vas men tut, tut men zich. Tut men gut, tut men zich; tut men shlecht, tut men zich* — What you do to others is done to you. If you treat others well, it's the same for you. But every time you try to hurt someone else, you only hurt yourself." I apparently didn't convince him, because when I once asked Mr. Singer, "How long are you going to continue your war with these people?" he answered,

"Azzoi lang vi ich vell leiben, de milchamah vet ongein — As long as I live, the war will go on!"

One Shabbos, in 1957, our whole Dorchester house was crammed full of guests for Reb Pinchas' *Bar Mitzvah*. It was so crowded that Rebbetzin Soroh Sashe had to move in with me, and the Rebbe had to sleep on the couch in his office. Mr. Singer, who was too busy to notice, later went into the Rebbe's dark office. When he saw someone sleeping on the Rebbe's couch, he was beside himself: *"Du legt min di schnorrers oichet* — They're putting the *schnorrers* (freeloaders) in here too!" The Rebbe woke up and thought it was funny; but Mr. Singer was even more upset that the Rebbe had given up his own bed. He really loved people in his own special way, but he definitely had his eccentricities.

Mr. Singer's Old Age

Although he used to grumble a bit, we took Mr. Singer's complaints with a grain of salt. We knew that he was actually kindhearted, faithful and all alone in the world. He had occasional visits from his somewhat religious sister-in-law and his nieces, but that was about it. His pleasures were few. I remember him enjoying his main *fleishig* meal every day at noontime: hot potatoes and a sliced raw onion. He ate all this together with *shmaltz* or oil, yet he lived to a ripe old age without ever once worrying about cholesterol!

One day, when Mr. Singer was 91 we took Rebbetzin Soroh Sashe to the airport so she could visit her children in New York. When we came home — we were already living in Brookline then — it was just starting to snow. Mr. Singer told us that he was going across the street to buy a newspaper. Although we didn't realize it, he didn't return. I thought he had come inside and gone to his room without our hearing him.

That night, at 9 p.m., we got a call from the hospital saying that Mr. Singer had been hit by a car. His X-rays revealed no broken bones; and the hospital asked us to come and take him home. Luckily, we had a small bedroom near the kitchen on the first floor.

We put him to bed there, but I soon noticed that he couldn't move from side to side. My son Pinchas and one of the college students who lived with us helped Mr. Singer all through the night, making him as comfortable as possible.

The next day, New Year's Day, I called our doctor, Dr. Arnold Starr. I told him, "I don't understand it. The hospital said the X-rays showed nothing wrong, but Mr. Singer can't move from side to side. It looks like one of his knees was hurt." Dr. Starr, a senior surgeon at the hospital, said, "Holiday or not, bring him right in. Don't even look at the head nurse. If she shouts at you, just say, 'He's Dr. Starr's patient.' " So I brought in Mr. Singer, and Dr. Starr took personal care of him.

When new X-rays were taken, the doctors found that Mr. Singer had indeed fractured one knee. They placed it in a temporary cast, and later sent Mr. Singer to a hospital for the chronically ill to recuperate completely. It turned out that Mr. Singer liked it there very much. There were no *meshulachim*, everyone spoke Yiddish, and he enjoyed three full meals a day. In fact, when he got better, he chose to stay there.

The Rebbe and I used to visit him quite often. The Rebbe's brother, Reb Moshe, also visited him when he came to Boston. On one such visit he asked Mr. Singer, "How are you?" and Mr. Singer told him, "*Az men laibt, darf men zien tzufreiden* — As long as you are still alive, you have to be satisfied." In fact, Mr. Singer lived at his hospital in quiet contentment for two more years, using his Social Security checks to pay for his stay. He passed away peacefully at the age of 93. For two whole generations he had been a loyal part of the family.

SIXTEEN

The College Connection

Dorchester Declines

In the early 1950s, the old "Jewish neighborhoods" of Roxbury and Dorchester began to change. It wasn't just a home here or there; entire organizations and communities moved. The Hebrew Teachers College left Dorchester for Brookline in 1953, and Dorchester's largest Conservative temple, Mishkan Tefillah, left for Newton a year later. We held on as long as we could — for eight more years — but our congregants kept leaving.

At first we only had to import people from Brookline to help make up our daily *Minchah minyan.* Then even the Shabbos *minyan* began to shrink. Eventually we had to move. It was sad to leave a place where we had lived and worked for 17 long years; but our move to Brookline, which brought us into closer contact with Boston's college community, was a turning point in Bostoner *Chassidus.*

Brookline

In Brookline we found a nice, large four-story townhouse on Beacon Street, a wide four-lane thoroughfare with tree-lined trolley tracks in the center. We and the trolley tracks are still there 34 years later, although most of the original trees have succumbed to Dutch elm disease. It is still a beautiful, refined neighborhood, with lots of *shuls,* schools and *Yiddin.* It's not a Jewish neighborhood in the New York sense, where almost everyone is Jewish, but we can still easily find whatever we need.

Relations with the non-Jewish community are pretty good too. One of our college student friends got thoroughly lost late one Simchas Torah night. Finally he met a red-haired Irish nurse, coming home from her hospital shift in her white uniform and shoes. He asked her, "How do you get to Brigham's Ice Cream Parlor [across the street from us] from here?" She took one look at his *yarmulke* and said, "Oh, you mean the Rebbe? First you go straight, then ..."

Our current home and New England Chassidic Center in Brookline, Massachusetts (a suburb of Boston) has been added to many times

The House

As you know by now, our house has to be more than a home. It also has to be a *shul, mikveh,* social hall and drop-in center. In short, every square inch is used, sometimes twice. The first floor of the New England Chassidic Center of 1710 Beacon Street houses the *shul.* Although a high *mechitzah* (partition) separates the women's section from the rest of the *shul,* we women can see everything just fine. The Rebbe had it made from "one-way" glass decorated with latticework. The second floor holds the Rebbe's study and large library, a small secretary's office, the kitchen and the dining room. The third floor has four bedrooms; and the fourth floor, three more. The basement houses the *mikveh* and, after subsequent remodeling, a social hall. In fact, the house has been added to several times, and is now one and a half times its original size.

Collegiates Move In

The Boston area is full of colleges — Harvard, M.I.T., Brandeis, Boston University, Northeastern, Wellesley and so on. There are about 130,000 college students in all, and many are Jewish. You wouldn't have thought that many of them would be interested in an "old-fashioned" Rebbe, and a rather uncompromising one at that. In fact, in Dorchester, we were "off the beaten path." Few students made the trek and fewer still stayed on. All this changed in Brookline, where we were within walking distance of several colleges and convenient to others.

A college student came to visit the Rebbe in 1962, shortly after our move, and was very impressed. He wanted to learn with the Rebbe on a regular basis; but the trip to and from his campus was too much for him. At that time we still had a very small congregation, and we were constantly worried that we wouldn't be able to find 10 men for a *minyan.* I suggested to the Rebbe that we rent out a room or two in our house to college students. This would guarantee us a *minyan,* while making it easier for the students to learn with the Rebbe.

This system worked just fine. The college boys had their own kitchen in the basement for weekdays, but on Shabbos and *Yom Tov* they ate with us. They enjoyed the atmosphere of being with the Rebbe so much that they began bringing their friends to stay with us for Shabbos. Since our "live-in" students were all from different colleges — one went to M.I.T., one went to Brandeis, another to Harvard — we soon began to attract quite a conglomeration of students from nearby schools. Then the newcomers began bringing other young men; and then young women began hearing about us, and we soon had our hands full. We packed the boys into the fourth-floor bedrooms, while the girls shared bedrooms with our daughters on the third floor. In fact, some of these girls became very close to our daughters, and to this day are still like extended family.

Some students even made the nine-mile walk to our home from Brandeis University in Waltham. On hot summer days, they would walk in after lunch and stay for *Shalosh Seudos.* During the afternoon, they were free to take fruits and cakes and whatever else they wanted from our refrigerator. This really bothered Mr. Singer. He resented all the young strangers "raiding" our refrigerator; but I told him that he should be used to running an open house by now.

Shabbatonim

Soon our house was full of students every Shabbos, and we had to place some of the overflow with local families. Every so often, we put up signs on local campuses announcing a Shabbaton. Then we would host 50 to 70 college students at a time. Some walked in from their campuses, some stayed with friends, some stayed with nearby families and the rest stayed with us. After Friday-night services they came upstairs for a communal supper. Since the Rebbe made *Kiddush* late, there was a relaxed hour or so for the students to talk with him and with each other. The Rebbe spoke at each meal, and there was lots of singing and good conversation.

Before we had the social hall, we had to improvise. The Rebbe's office and the living room became the men's dining room, while the women used the regular dining room. We had to set up mirrors so that the women could see what was going on in the men's section, although everything could be heard. Later, we extended the basement and converted it into our "Sharzer Hall." We also extended the second floor to create an extra large dining room next to our kitchen. We called it "The Sukkah Dining Room" because it has a special *sukkah* roof for Sukkos, and a sliding regular roof for use during the rest of the year.

Of course, the young people came not only for the food, but for the spiritual nourishment as well. They would talk freely to the Rebbe about their personal lives and problems. After they became religious, many students would ask for advice on how to get along with their non-religious parents. The Rebbe always advised the students to go slow and to keep up a good relationship with their parents. They didn't have to change the whole world on their first Shabbos visit home! In general, the Rebbe has always preferred a slow but steady approach; it usually gives more lasting results.

I remember one set of parents who were extremely upset that their oldest son had become religious through the Rebbe. This lasted until their second son went off to join some guru in the Himalaya Mountains! Then they called and begged the Rebbe to influence their second son as he had their first. Their second son actually did come and spend some time with us. He did not become as observant as his brother, but he did develop a great love and respect for *Yiddishkeit.*

The Sixties

In the '60s and '70s, a lot of Jewish youngsters began searching for their Jewish "roots" and we opened a part-time *yeshivah* for them. To this day, my youngest son, Rav Naftali, gives special classes for the college students: a *Daf Yomi shiur,* a *Gemara shiur* and a *shiur* between *Minchah* and *Maariv.*

Some of the college students in those days were real activists. One group even threatened to take over the microphone at a UJA Dinner if they wouldn't let them *bentch* (say the Grace After Meals). As one of them later said, "What would they have done? Arrest us for praying?" They made a peculiar contrast to the Rebbe, who is always calm, relaxed and avoids confrontation. They wore long hair, he wore *peyos.* They wore suits or jeans; he wore a long black coat and a wide-brimmed black hat. They were from a generation that was "doing its own thing," and he made it clear from the beginning that the Torah is timeless, that it has rules and that he follows all of them. He wasn't interested in compromises or an easy way out, no matter what that did to his "popularity." In short, he was a Rebbe.

Somehow, the combination worked out just fine. Everyone knows the truth when he hears it, and the students appreciated his honesty (they called it "authenticity"). When the first edition of *A Student's Guide to Jewish Boston* came out, the Combined Jewish Philanthropies of Boston, who funded it, were probably quite surprised to see that the student editors had dedicated it to the Bostoner Rebbe and put a full-page picture of the Rebbe inside. The calendar in the back even listed the Rebbe's birthday as one of its "important events." Most of these students are still *frum* today and raising lovely families.

From the students, the Rebbe learned a lot about the disappointments and frustrations of life in the secular world. He also found out more about "the system." One science student told the Rebbe that his professor had warned his group not to give out any research "secrets" when they met with other scientists. The Rebbe was shocked to hear that potentially life-saving facts were being withheld just so each scientist could get his own share of the credit. What about the people who died or suffered meanwhile?

Baruch Hashem, we have been fortunate with our *baalei teshuvah.* At first, many parents worried that their newly religious children would sit and learn Torah all day and be unable to earn a *parnasah.* Their fears were unfounded. All the college students I have kept up with have turned out to be capable, self-sufficient breadwinners. They have been community conscious too. Once, when the Rebbe and I were visiting a large city in Israel, we found that three of our former students were the presidents of their local *mikveh* organizations.

Work and More Work

The *Shabbatonim* were a big hit from the very start, full of *ruach* and singing and the beauty of Shabbos. Few people, however, realized the tremendous amount of effort it took to make things seem effortless.

The college men soon found out that the Rebbe could speak to them about almost anything: Torah topics, *hashkafah,* the latest news, their studies. In this way, the Rebbe developed a wonderful rapport with these young men. The Rebbe would ask me if I spoke that way with the women, but I was usually too busy just preparing and serving all the food to do as much with the women as he did with the men. It was like hosting a *Sheva Brachos* every Shabbos. Even when I had a "small" crowd, there were 25 to 30 guests, who all had to be fed at the same time.

We had to set up tables every Friday afternoon for the Friday night *tish,* serve each course, clean up, wash the dishes and then, late at night, set up the shul's *Kiddush* for the next morning. The lunchtime *seudah* upstairs the next day was the same thing all over again: set up, serve, clean up. The *Shalosh Seudos* for men was served downstairs in the *shul* itself, while the women ate upstairs. The *Motzaei Shabbos Melaveh Malkah* drew a much smaller crowd; and we usually just served leftover *cholent, kugel* and herring. I usually made a *parve cholent* for Shabbos, so anyone who wanted to stay *parve* after the *Melaveh Malkah* could do so.

I had to cook in huge quantities and do almost everything myself. College students can sometimes be a bit self-centered — it's probably part of growing up — and they usually did not help with the cooking or the cleaning up. Dishwashing was particularly difficult on Friday nights, because we could only use cold water, which is freezing in the winter. I remember one *Shabbaton* evening when a group of college girls were sitting at my kitchen table talking while I worked. I put down two towels and said, "I hope you girls don't mind wiping while I sit down for awhile too." I don't think they understood that I was simply exhausted!

Before plastic plates and dishes became part of our lives, I used to wash our Shabbos dishes until Tuesday. You can count the crockery yourself: 50 fish plates, 50 soup plates, 50 large meat plates, 50 knives, 100 forks (fish and meat must be kept separate), 50 spoons, 50 glasses and then *Kiddush* cups, platters, pots, pans and serving pieces, all done *twice* (for the two major meals). Then there were two smaller meals! When I moved from Dorchester to Brookline, the woman who helped me in the house warned that, if we didn't get an automatic dishwasher, she was quitting!

I did try to get some extra household help for Friday nights, but this never worked out well. The non-Jewish maids resented seeing the large Jewish dinners. I would invite them to come sit with us, but they would refuse. The Jewish maids resented that none of our young guests were helping with the work.

People talk to me a lot about the "drudgery" and "exploitation" of those days, but I don't see it that way. A Jewish husband and wife are a team with something important to do in this world. If I didn't do what I do, the Rebbe couldn't do what he does. Just imagine how happy I was to see our Shabbos table full of beautiful young students coming closer to the Rebbe and Torah. And think how happy I was to see them grow and develop, to see that we had made a difference.

Since many newly religious girls didn't have a mother nearby, I often became their role model in many aspects of *Yiddishkeit*. In our home, they learned the beauty of lighting Shabbos candles, the excitement of a *Shabbos tish* and the hustle and bustle that went into preparing it.

Once another Rebbetzin asked me, regarding all our *kiruv* work with the college students, "What do you do it for? What do you need it for?" I told her that I do it *l'shem Shamayim* (for the sake of Heaven), because these students are searching. They are innocent and wandering, and can become lost if we don't show them the way. We have found that the best way, perhaps the only way, to bring students closer to *Yiddishkeit* is to treat them like members of our own family. That is how Bostoner *Chassidus* was built, one Jew at a time.

How I Began Using Paper Plates

One young woman did help me a great deal running the household, and we became quite close. She was almost like another daughter. Eventually she became engaged to a brilliant young man, who also went to Brandeis, and together they used to attend Rav Yosef Ber Soloveitchik's public *Motzaei Shabbos shiurim* on the *sedrah* of the week. The young man was exceptionally bright and used to answer all of the Rav's questions.

In fact, Rav Soloveitchik once spoke to the Rebbe about this wonderful young man. Then the Rebbe mentioned all the trouble his fiancée was having with her parents, since they did not keep a kosher home. Rav Soloveitchik was so concerned that he personally rode out to visit her startled parents and explained the importance of *kashrus* to them!

Later, the young couple were invited to Rav Soloveitchik's home for Shabbos. I asked my young friend what Shabbos was like there. "It was very similar to Shabbos at the Rebbe's," she said. "They sing the same *zemiros* and the Rav says a *dvar Torah.* About the only difference I could see is that they use paper plates. Rebbetzin Soloveitchik doesn't want to have too many dishes to wash after Shabbos, because she likes to attend the Rav's *Motzaei Shabbos shiur* herself."

That was interesting news! I went right into the Rebbe's office and told him. "I am busy washing our Shabbos dishes until Tuesday. Why can't I use paper plates too? I'll serve you on china plates but, *kein ayin hara*, when we have 30 to 40 guests, I'm so busy that I don't even have time to talk with them!" The Rebbe agreed and said, "By all means. Go ahead and use paper plates for the guests if you want," and that became my system from then on. I have always been grateful to that young woman who told me about Rebbetzin Soloveitchik's great idea.

This young woman later told me that she now finds it easy to prepare Shabbos for her own large family because she learned everything from me: bake ahead of time, don't make too great a variety and don't make the preparations too overwhelming. She makes just gefilte fish, chopped eggs (for Shabbos lunch), *cholent*, roast beef, fruit and cake.

A Recipe for Yerushalmi Kugel

I also found a shortcut for making *Yerushalmi kugel,* a dark-brown sweet and peppery noodle pudding. It was very popular in the old Jewish community of Jerusalem at the turn of the century, since it could be cooked on the top of a primus burner (few people had ovens). It is still popular today, although it is somewhat difficult to make. First you have to caramelize sugar in hot oil, pour the hot mixture over the cooked noodles and then fry it some more. Caramelizing the sugar is a tricky, and occasionally dangerous, business. After my oldest daughter-in-law burned her hand making it, I decided to experiment with different, less dramatic methods. Now, I simply use brown sugar instead.

To each package of cooked noodles, add four eggs, half a glass of oil, a flat teaspoon of salt, a half teaspoon of pepper (far more if you're *Yerushalmi*), two tablespoons of brown sugar, and a handful of flour. Mix all the ingredients together, pour them into a greased pan and bake the whole thing at 400 degrees for about 25 minutes. And there you have your *kugel*!

Shidduchim

Having 20 to 30 young men and 20 to 30 young women over for meals each Shabbos, I soon found myself busy making *shidduchim* between them. This became even easier once we opened a part-time *yeshivah* for boys and a part-time seminary for girls. With Hashem's help, I was pretty successful. Many of the couples we helped bring together have already had their first grandchildren.

One case that comes to mind involved a *ger tzedek,* a wonderful person who became interested in Judaism after the Six Day War. He was influenced by a new rabbi in his town, one of our own *baalei teshuvah.* After his conversion, he moved to Baltimore, attended *yeshivah* and then went into business. People always used to ask me if I knew of a *shidduch* for him. Finally, I *redd* (suggested) a *shidduch* for him with one of our Boston girls. At first he was reluctant to come meet her. He asked his married friends if it would really be worth traveling all the way to Boston. They told him, "The Rebbetzin made our *shidduchim* and, if I were you, I'd take the next train to Boston!" He did and the *shidduch* turned out nicely. They married and now have a lovely family.

Another college student had dated the same girlfriend since he had been a young boy. When she decided to drop him — people do change as they grow older — he was devastated. He dropped out of school and even started taking drugs. At this point, somebody brought him in to see the Rebbe. The Rebbe sent him for psychiatric treatment and then encouraged him to get a job. When he recovered, we helped him enroll in another university and to get on with making a life for himself. Today, our young friend is happily married, living in Israel and working successfully in his own business.

When Things Go Wrong

Most of our own *shidduchim* worked out just fine, *Baruch Hashem,* but not all marriages do. This can create a lot of problems, since a Jewish marriage is a strong bond that can only be ended by a *get,* a formal writ of divorce. Otherwise the couple is still married according to Jewish law, no matter what secular laws say. If the woman remarries, she is committing adultery; and her children from her second, adulterous marriage will be *mam-*

zeirim, unable to marry a properly born Jew. The *mamzer* may be a fine person, and his parents' misbehavior is obviously not his fault, but the same applies to all other birth defects — deafness, blindness and so on. The problem remains a problem.

One of our newly religious college students, a young woman, was the child of her mother's second marriage. Her father was a non-Jewish professor at a nearby college. One weekend, she heard a visiting rabbi speak about the problem of *mamzeirus.* She was devastated and called the Rebbe Saturday night, crying that she must be a *mamzer,* since her mother had never received a *get* from her first husband. The Rebbe told her that since her father was not Jewish, her mother's second "marriage" was not a Jewish marriage at all. Although she was born out of wedlock, she was certainly not a *mamzeres.* This young woman had always felt terrible about her father not being Jewish, but she now understood that, in her case, it was actually a great *chessed.*

Getting a Get

Of course the best solution is to stop such problems before they can start. That means making sure that all secularly divorced couples also have a formal Jewish divorce. The Rebbe has been yelled at more than once for "meddling," but he realizes how important a *get* can be for the couple's subsequent children.

Once a woman came to the Rebbe and begged him to help her get a Jewish divorce from her ex-husband. He had been a college professor in California, but the Rebbe soon found out that he was no longer there. Eventually the Rebbe traced him to a university in Connecticut. When the Rebbe called him, he refused to give his ex-wife a *get* unless the Rebbe would promise him that he would find another nice woman to marry. The Rebbe had no choice but to give him a *brachah.* Later, the Rebbe underwent emergency surgery in New York and was recuperating at his brother's home. The phone rang and it was this same man. He was getting married to a fine young woman and wanted to thank the Rebbe for his *brachah.*

Some husbands are even less cooperative. We used to have a

good friend in Boston who supplied the *shul* with occasional groceries. Unfortunately, his son refused to give his wife a Jewish divorce, which meant that she could never remarry. The Rebbe advised her that, in her civil divorce case, she should insist on getting a Jewish divorce before the civil divorce went through. The Rebbe even went to court and gave testimony about the case himself. We lost the groceries; but we were happy that the woman finally got her Jewish divorce.

Another young wife came to the Rebbe with a similar problem. Her husband, a psychiatrist, refused to give her a Jewish divorce. She expected the Rebbe to give her some special prayers or *Tehillim* to recite, but instead he gave her some practical advice. "Has your husband passed his Psychiatric Board Exams yet?" the Rebbe asked.

"No."

"Then warn your husband that if he doesn't give you a Jewish divorce you will go to the Board and complain about his mental cruelty."

She did what the Rebbe told her, and her husband agreed to give her a Jewish divorce five minutes later.

Of course, in a functioning Torah society, all these shenanigans would not be necessary. If a husband tried to hurt his wife by refusing to give her a *get,* he would simply be thrown in jail until he changed his mind. Nowadays, it takes a lot of tact and intelligence just to get people to do the right thing.

SEVENTEEN

Branches

With all this discussion about other people's families, I might as well tell you something about my own. A *tzaddik* is supposed to love everyone else's children as much as his own, but I must confess to more than a little favoritism. Still, I will keep this section very brief. If I talk too much about my children, I will have to let you take out your pictures and give you equal time.

Reb Pinchas Dovid

The Rebbe and I have five children, *kein ayin hara,* three boys and two girls. Our eldest son, Pinchas Dovid, was named after the Rebbe's father. He looks a great deal like him; and he inherited his grandfather's *mesiras nefesh* for learning as well. Pinchas was born in 1944, just before we left New York City for Boston.

Since Pinchas was our *bechor* (firstborn), he set the pattern for all our sons' education. When he was four, he went to kindergarten at the local Jewish day school. His first day, however, got off to a rough start. *Chassidim* don't even cut their sons' hair until they are three; then they cut it all very short except for two long *peyos* (side-curls) which are left untouched. One of the teachers at the school took one look at Pinchas' long *peyos* and put him in with the girls! Now, *Baruch Hashem,* Boston has a traditional *cheder* and *peyos* are no longer a strange sight.

At home we spoke only Yiddish to the children. Our Yiddish was so pure and "European" that once, when we were all traveling to New York City by train, a woman asked me if *"Du bist itst arup fun shif* — Did you just got off the boat from Europe?" The language gap also created problems for Pinchas, since all his teachers and classmates spoke only English. Finally, we started speaking English to our children, and they soon started speaking English too.

Once things got straightened out, Pinchas did very well at school but, when he turned nine, he faced another problem. His New York relatives were already beginning to learn *Gemara* in their *chedarim* and, if he remained in Boston, he would fall further and further behind. He asked us to let him go to learn at Torah Vodaath in New York! We all told him that he was still far too young; but Pinchas was determined and, eventually, we gave in. It wasn't easy. I felt like Channah, the mother of Shmuel *HaNavi,* who had to send her young son away to serve Hashem. The day Pinchas left, I found him crying, overwhelmed by the whole thing. I gently suggested that he stay in Boston with me; but he just said, "Don't look at my tears, Mommy. I have to keep up with other children my age."

Torah Vodaath didn't have a dormitory in those days, so Pinchas first stayed with my sister, Rebbetzin Chaya Yehudis, and brother-in-law, the Clevelander-Strozhinitzer Rebbe, in their apartment over the Clevelander Shul. Although we had family in New York, being away from home at such a young age was pretty traumatic for him and for all our other sons, who followed in his footsteps; but they all stuck it out and succeeded beyond our highest hopes.

Pinchas learned very well at Torah Vodaath and, in 1962, at age 17, he left for Israel to study at the Ponovez Yeshivah in Bnei Brak. I visited him in Israel later that year. It was my first trip to Israel and a very exciting experience. In 1964 Reb Pinchas returned to America to learn at the Beis Medrash Govoha in Lakewood, New Jersey, where he eventually became known as a *talmid chacham* and *mechadesh.*

Reb Pinchas, our oldest son, married Sarah Greenwald (left). Here I'm talking to her sister and my daughter Shayna (far right)

Impressed with Pinchas' character, the Chuster Rav, one of the great *gedolim* and *poskim* to survive the *Churban* in Europe, chose Pinchas as the husband for his daughter, Sarah Beila Greenwald. When the Chuster Rav heard that Pinchas was born in 1944, he began to tremble. He could hardly believe that during the very year that the Nazis, *yimach shemam* (may their names be erased), were destroying Chust and the other Jewish communities of Czechoslovakia, Hashem, in His Mercy, was already arranging for the future, preparing a husband for his daughter in faraway America.

Perhaps because of his suffering at the hands of the Nazis, the Chuster Rav passed away at a relatively young age, and Reb Pinchas was chosen as his successor. He now heads the Chuster *Kehillah* in Boro Park, where he is also heavily involved in *chessed* and *kashrus* work. There he founded Chai Lifeline, Camp Simcha (which helps children with cancer) and founded Nachas Healthnet (which provides health and support services for the needy) which he now heads.

Reb Mayer Alter

When I was expecting for the second time, a friend predicted, "This time you are going to have a little girl"; but I told her, "No, I'm going to have another boy." Since my first pregnancy had been very difficult, however, I became worried about the future. I was greatly reassured when my stepfather, the Clevelander Rebbe, came to me in a dream and told me, "Don't worry. This time, it will be much easier." That same night, I dreamt that I was entering a beautiful, large *shul.* The Rav was saying that a very great *neshamah,* a big guest, was coming. I turned around and saw a beautiful little boy with blond curls. Then I dreamt a third dream. I had given birth to a boy. My stepfather, Rav Mayer Leifer, the Clevelander Rebbe, and my *zeide,* Rav Alter Ze'ev, the

Our oldest children, Pinchas, Shayna, and Mayer

Stryzover Rebbe, came to the *bris* and said, *"Mazal tov."* So I named my second son Mayer Alter after them.

Mayer was a cheerful, happy child. He was also very concerned for others. One day, when he was six, he came home with his glasses broken. He saw one boy starting to hit another and quickly stuck his own head in the way to prevent the first boy from being hurt.

Mayer's education resembled Pinchas': the local Jewish day school, then Torah Vodaath, Ponovez and Lakewood. Back home, he showed his great talent as an organizer. His dream was to start a *cheder* in Boston. When he didn't find enough support in the community, he supported it himself. Now, *Baruch Hashem,* Boston's *cheder* is thriving with over 180 children. Many boys have *peyos,* and the girls dress with true *tznius.*

Reb Mayer is now the Rav of the Bostoner community in Har Nof, a large new religious suburb on the west side of Jerusalem. There he continues to organize new Torah organizations, activities and facilities for the wider community. Reb Mayer's Rebbetzin, Sima Mossberg, is the daughter of a European *talmid chacham* who moved to New York. She was deeply involved in the ROFEH medical support project in Boston and continues her Rofeh *chessed* and community work in Har Nof.

Rebbetzin Shayna Gitel

Before I even knew that I was expecting my third child, I dreamt that I was teasing my mother-in-law, saying, "You always give me a *brachah* that I should have boys. This time I'm going to have a girl, your first granddaughter." When Rebbetzin Soroh Sashe heard about my dream, she told me, "Well, if you do have a girl, I would very much like her to be named after my mother, Gitel." On the other hand, since her mother had passed away at the young age of 49, she told me to combine Gitel with another name.

That very night, I dreamt that Rebbetzin Shayna Elka, the Rebbe's father's mother, who had lived in *Eretz Yisrael* many years ago, had come to America and traveled to Boston just to see me. She was wearing an old-fashioned outfit, with flowing skirts, just as women wore at the turn-of-the-century. I had heard much about this great *tzadekes,* but I had never met her. Finally, I dreamt again that I gave birth to a girl. I took this as a *siman* (sign) and later named my new daughter after both great-grandmothers: Shayna Gitel.

For many years Shayna shared a room with Rebbetzin Soroh Sashe, and they became very close. The Rebbetzin's intense approach to *tefillah* and *mitzvos* made a powerful, lifelong impression on Shayna. When Shayna lost her first tooth, her grandmother told her, "I lost my last tooth after my wedding!" This was quite true, as Rebbetzin Soroh Sashe had been engaged at six and had married at twelve-and-a-half.

Shayna married Rav Yosef Frankel, the Vyelipoler Rav and *Rosh Yeshivah* of the Vyelipoler Yeshivah in Brooklyn. She now teaches a *tefillah* class at a Jewish girls high school, where she tries to transmit the love of *tefillah* she learned from her family, especially her grandmothers.

My Life in the Balance

There are five years between Shayna Gitel and my youngest son, Rav Naftali. Unfortunately, during those years, I was very ill, suffering from untreated bleeding ulcers. Since I am fair skinned and have a pinkish complexion, doctors just assumed that my constant complaints were psychological not physical. They never really took me seriously. When I had trouble with my veins, a circulation specialist prescribed Darvon and aspirin. I told him that I couldn't take aspirin, because I had trouble with my stomach, but he insisted. His treatment further aggravated the ulcer no one believed I had.

My most serious attack began one *Erev Shabbos* in 1949. Preparing the meals took all my strength. By *Shalosh Seudos,* I didn't even have the strength to sit at the table. *Motzaei Shabbos* I had a terrible headache. It was so severe that I could not even speak to my mother or mother-in-law on the telephone. I took aspirin for the headache, but that just further aggravated the ulcer.

I fainted three days in a row and, on the third day, I ran a high fever and vomited. I lay in bed feeling deathly ill. When our family doctor came, I told him that I was fainting; but he didn't take that seriously either. I looked in the mirror and saw that I was as white as a sheet. I remembered that my stepfather, Rav Leifer, was anemic when he became this pale, so I asked the doctor to test my blood. He shrugged it off and said that, when I felt better, he would test me in his office. After he left I felt so ill that I could not see clearly. I had to grope around and feel the walls in order to walk the short distance from the bathroom to our bedroom. Suddenly I said, "I can't see," and fell down in a faint.

This was all in the middle of July. My sister, Chaya Yehudis, then a high school student on summer vacation, had come to visit us and help with the children. She and the Rebbe threw cold water on me and got me back into bed. The mirror was opposite my bed, and I could see again that I was terribly pale. I told them, "I am sure that it's my stomach. Call Dr. Dubins. He treated my mother-in-law for her gall bladder, and I remember he was very sympathetic."

Dr. Dubins, who had a waiting room full of patients, excused himself and came straight to my bedside. He literally saved my life. Within five minutes he had made his diagnosis. He said that I was bleeding internally, that the situation was serious, and that I had to be hospitalized at once. My sister said, "Maybe I should make her a glass of orange juice to give her strength?" "G-d forbid! You can't give her anything!" he said. He was going to take me to the hospital himself but, when I fainted again on the way downstairs, he said that he didn't want to risk the trip alone. He called an ambulance and I was rushed to the hospital.

The doctors who examined me in the hospital told the Rebbe that I was bleeding internally. They drew a bit of blood to find out my blood type and said that I would receive a transfusion within an hour. They told the Rebbe that he could go home and take care of the family; but I felt terribly ill and I asked the Rebbe to stay with me.

After the doctors went away, I suddenly felt a numbness in my head, arms and feet and a piercing pain throughout my body. I asked the Rebbe to say *Viduy* (final confession) with me. Instead, he ran to get the nurse, who took my blood pressure and ran to call the doctors back. Meanwhile, she sent a nurse's aide to take care of me. I told her to get me some crushed ice. I had had a lot of experience with my stepfather and whenever he was that ill, we used to put ice on his chest and arms. I also put some ice on my lips. It really helped relieve the shock.

The doctors and nurses came running with blood transfusions and oxygen. They told the Rebbe, "She'll accept the blood within 20 minutes or she'll be gone. The veins and arteries are starting to close." Dr. Dubins later told me that they all regretted not seeing how serious my case was during their examination, just moments before.

The Rebbe had telephoned my mother when I was rushed to the hospital. Later she told us that, the night before my attack, she had dreamt that my father, Rav Naftali Ungar, and the Rebbe's father, Rav Pinchas Dovid, were together in a big room pacing the floor, wringing their hands and praying. We understood that they must have sensed the danger and intervened for me in Heaven.

I survived the attack, *Baruch Hashem,* but I had gone into shock and lost a lot of strength in my muscles. My recuperation lasted almost a full year. Just making a bed, sweeping a floor or lifting the smallest thing was enough to exhaust me. It was difficult to manage the household tasks, but we couldn't have help 24 hours a day and, with three small children, there was always work to be done.

Reb Naftali

When I was expecting our youngest son, I dreamt that the Rebbe and I had gone to visit my father, Rav Naftali Ungar, and his father, Rav Yehudah Ungar, the Sokolover Rebbe. The Rebbe and I were together in a beautiful elevator with lovely metal flowers. Up and up we went. Finally we came to a large hall where people had gathered for a *seudas mitzvah.* Outside the hall there were open display cases full of blue hats decorated with blue feathers. I tried on a hat and then put it back. We walked into the hall for the *seudas mitzvah,* and my father, Rav Naftali, came to greet us. He took the Rebbe over to his table and asked him to sit beside my *zeide,* Rav Yehudah Ungar. "No, *Shver,*" the Rebbe answered. "You are older and should go ahead of me. You sit first and then I will sit." Rav Naftali turned to his father and said proudly, "You see what *kavod* my son-in-law gives me?"

Meanwhile, I went into the women's section. After the *seudah,* everyone *bentched,* and I went to meet the Rebbe to go back downstairs. Outside the hall, I tried on one of the hats again and wanted to take one with me. Just then, someone called me over and said, "*Kim aher, ying viebul* — Come here, young woman. You can't take anything back down from here." So I put the hat back, and the Rebbe and I went back into the elevator. When I woke up, I immediately suspected that I was expecting again and, sure enough, I was. I named our new son Naftali Yehudah, after my father and *zeide* who had appeared to me in the dream.

The Wednesday night before Naftali Yehudah was born, I dreamt that I would give birth to a boy on Friday. This didn't give me much time. Rebbetzin Soroh Sashe was away in the country, so all day Thursday I baked *challos* and cakes and prepared for Shabbos. By the time I got into bed late Thursday night, my legs were swollen and my feet were aching. Then I had to go back downstairs to the kitchen, because an unexpected guest had arrived who needed to be fed. After I served him supper, I went upstairs again and went into labor.

I didn't want to go to the hospital too early, so I got up and ironed all the clothes I could, so that the children would have them ready for the rest of the week. I let the Rebbe rest until about 3 a.m. and then we went to the hospital. I had our baby two hours later.

The family soon mobilized to take my place. The Rebbe's brother, the Bostoner Rebbe of New York, had rented a little place in Cohasset, an oceanside resort outside Boston, for the summer. When his Rebbetzin heard that I had given birth, she came in

Friday morning and prepared the rest of the Shabbos meals; and Rebbetzin Soroh Sashe returned from the country on Sunday to help with the house and the children.

Why hadn't I named one of my earlier children Naftali? My father had been shot by the Nazis during the war, but we had no confirmation of this for a long time. True, my father had come to me in a dream and told me what had happened to him, and I even had asked him for *mechilah* in my dream. Still, I did not really want to believe that he had died, so I gave other names to my first sons. By the time Naftali was born we had learned that my dreams about my father had been all too true.

Naftali always wanted to be a teacher. Once a doctor came to visit us and asked him, "Naftali, what do you want to be when you grow up?" "A teacher," he said. After the doctor came out of Rebbetzin Soroh Sashe's room, he asked Naftali, "Why a teacher? Why not a rabbi like your father?" Little Naftali answered him, "You know, a rabbi is a teacher!"

Rav Naftali followed in the footsteps of his brothers: Boston's Jewish Day School and then Torah Vodaath. When he left for New York, I still felt an ache like Channah but I was, at least, already

The women of the family gather at Reb Naftali's Bar Mitzvah. From far left to right: my sister-in-law, the Bostoner Rebbetzin of New York; Rebbetzin Sarah Sasha, the Rebbe's mother; myself; my mother, the Clevelander-Nadvorner Rebbetzin, and my sister Chaya Yehudis (1965)

prepared for it. Although Naftali had Pinchas and Mayer for support, he was much younger and they both left New York when he was 11. He missed everyone terribly and eventually transferred to the Philadelphia Yeshivah. There, he thrived under Rav Shmuel Kamenetsky, *Shlita.* He went on to learn at Ponovez and Lakewood, before returning to Boston.

Reb Naftali married Shaindy Weiss, daughter of Rav Shalom Weiss, the Uhela Rav, *Shlita.* Reb Naftali is now the Rav of the Bostoner community in Boston and New England. This involves simultaneously handling the *shul,* the college students, ROFEH and everything else that comes his way. This is particularly difficult during the half year that the Rebbe and I spend in Israel.

Rebbetzin Tobeh Leah

Two years later, I was expecting my youngest daughter. I had been very close to my sister, Leah, who had been killed with her whole family in Poland during the war. All efforts to bring her to America had failed. One night I dreamt that Leah had come to live with us in America and was happy. Then I knew that

Our younger children, Reb Naftali and Tobeh Leah (c. 1958)

I would give birth to a girl. We combined Leah's name with Tobeh, the name of my father's mother. Tobeh is also the name of the Rebbe's great-grandmother, the mother of Reb Shmuel Shmelke.

Toby, as we called her, had a heart of gold. She was always giving her toys away to the other children. Toby also loved helping guests. When my mother got sick, I had to rush to New York. Shayna had already married and left home, so Toby took over and ran the whole Shabbos herself, guests and all. Then she took over running a 60-person wedding reception for a *kallah* I had befriended. Some of her friends were supposed to help, but the *kallah* got nervous at the last minute, and they had to sit with her and hold her hand. Toby did a great job, although she was only 16.

Toby also went to Boston's Lubavitch girls' school through 12th grade. Then she learned in Israel for a year at Bais Yaakov Yerushalayim (commonly known as "BJJ"). She married Rav Moshe Chaim Geldzahler, the son of Rav Yehoshua Geldzahler, the *menahel* and founder of Yeshivah Toras Yisroel of Queens. Her hus-

In 1969 Reb Moshe Shimon, Reb Pinchas' oldest son (now a Rav) enjoyed the attention due an oldest grandson

band is also a grandson of Rav Eliyahu Dessler, the *Michtav M'Eliyahu,* the well-known Gateshead *Rosh Kollel* and Ponovez *Mashgiach.* Toby and Reb Moshe Chaim first lived in Monsey, while he taught at Yeshivah Toras Yisroel. They now live in Har Nof, where Reb Moshe Chaim is the Rav of Bais Shlomo d'Boston, a second Bostoner *shul.*

. . . And on

Baruch Hashem, our children have all had children and we are now beginning to see great-grandchildren. It's quite a thrill. They visit us regularly and several now live or learn in Israel. In fact, Reb Pinchas' eldest son, Reb Moshe Shimon, and his family have moved to Har Nof, where he is a *Moreh Tzedek* in the main Bostoner *shul.* It's lovely seeing our family grow; and we are so grateful to Hashem for giving us such *Yiddishe nachas* from them all.

EIGHTEEN

The Medical Connection

Early Days

Another important part of our life in Boston was our medical support work. It began back during our early days in Dorchester, when the Rebbe's brother, and other *Rabbanim,* started sending people to Boston's famous medical centers for treatment. We tried to provide these patients and their families with both physical support (most lived with us) and with emotional and religious support. We also helped them find the right doctors and undergo treatment.

Several early cases stand out in my mind. My brother-in-law once sent us a *yeshivah bachur* who suffered from severe colitis. He had to have a colostomy operation but, at that time, Boston's hospitals did not provide kosher meals. I used to make him meals at home and bring them to him in the hospital every day. He was only 17 years old, far from home, and very depressed. The Rebbe and I invited his parents to stay with us for Pesach. This impressed us with the importance of providing support to the patients' families as well.

Later, a beautiful six-year-old boy moved in with us for several months. He was suffering from leukemia. On Shabbos, when I served *Kiddush* in *shul,* he loved helping me bring the wine, plates and forks. Mr. Singer used to yell at me for feeding him before feeding my baby daughter; but he came back famished from radiation treatment and my heart went out to him. He was cared for very well by Dr. Sidney Farber, founder of the Dana-Farber Cancer Center in Boston, but at that time, there was still no cure for childhood leukemia and our lovely little friend passed away.

The Rebbe, of course, provided other kinds of help as well. Once a five-year-old girl with a hole between the chambers of her heart came to Boston for open-heart surgery, together with her mother. Both of them stayed with us throughout the treatment. Unfortunately, right after the operation, X-rays showed that the hole had reopened. Her doctors wanted to operate again, but the specialists we consulted said that the risk of her dying from the second operation was 50 percent. The Rebbe talked to the mother and convinced her to wait until the doctors developed a better treatment.

Nine years later, the Boston Children's Hospital contacted the girl and asked her again to come for the operation. By this time, heart and lung machines had been developed, and the operation had a much better chance of success. The mother stayed with us over Shabbos. Just before the surgery she became intensely frightened, in fact, hysterical, and wanted to call the hospital to cancel the operation — all this while I was in the middle of preparing a *kiddush* for the *aufruf* for one of the *baalei teshuvah* who lived with us. It wasn't easy taking care of everything that Shabbos. The girl did undergo the surgery and the operation was, *Baruch Hashem,* successful. Eventually, she married and had children, and today she is a grandmother!

I have always been interested in medicine, perhaps because of all my respiratory problems as a child, and I was always interested in health and science in school. If I had not been a *Rebbeshe* daughter, I might have considered becoming a doctor.

Confronting Cancer

Cancer was even more of a problem in those days than it is today. A lovely couple we know had two beautiful daughters. The husband was studying in college and his wife was expecting their third child. When she encountered severe complications, her doctors just recommended bed rest; but two days later the husband called the Rebbe long distance. The Rebbe told him to have his wife's blood tested. Her doctors did so and discovered that she had a fast-growing cancer. The husband again telephoned the Rebbe, who insisted that the woman have both chemotherapy and radiation treatments. Since she was in her late 20s, with many childbearing years ahead, the doctors ignored the Rebbe's advice and tried radiation treatments without chemotherapy. This left some cancer cells untouched and, a year later, she developed a tumor in her lung. The Rebbe reassured her husband, "She still has a chance if they give her chemotherapy now. It's not too late." They did and she recovered completely. In fact, despite her doctors' worries, she later gave birth to another six gorgeous children.

The Rebbe had been involved in a similar case before but, unfortunately, one with a tragic ending. A young mother of three gave birth to a stillborn child. Afterwards, she experienced a great deal of pain and other complications. Her husband went to the Rebbe who asked me, "Is it natural for a woman to feel this way after giving birth?" When I told him no, the Rebbe sent her to specialists who discovered that she had a severe case of cancer. When I visited her in the hospital, she told me sadly, "All my life, I've been so careful about *kashrus;* but now I have to receive blood transfusions into my body whether the blood is kosher or not." It was too late to save her but, because of her sad story, the Rebbe became immediately suspicious of cancer in the case of the second woman.

Rofeh

For many years the Rebbe and I continued helping people this way but eventually, as Boston's medical centers and the Rebbe's services became better known, it became too much for us to handle by ourselves. The Rebbe decided to start a special organization to provide support services — advice, transportation, translators, kosher food, housing and moral support — for the many religious patients and their families who came to Boston each month. The Rebbe named the new organization ROFEH, the Hebrew word for doctor. In English, the letters spell out ROFEH's purpose: "Reaching Out, Furnishing Emergency Health Care."

ROFEH advises people where to turn for the best possible treatment for any illness. To do this, the Rebbe has built up an exceptionally close relationship with doctors and medical experts in Boston and throughout the country. An Israeli doctor we know did his postgraduate work in Boston. Once he was looking for the best doctor to consult for a particular illness. Another doctor told him: "Don't bother looking it up. Just call the ROFEH office and ask the Bostoner Rebbe. He'll tell you the name of the best doctor in the field." Out of curiosity this doctor did call the Rebbe, and the Rebbe gave him the same name that he had come up with after weeks of intensive research.

Many of the doctors the Rebbe stays in touch with are non-Jewish. All are leaders in their field, and several are Nobel Prize winners. The Rebbe has no problems talking to them, since he speaks a clear American English, has learned a great deal about medicine and doesn't waste their time. They often tell him, "Please ask the other rabbis not to call us; we just don't have the time for long discussions." Some of the other doctors on the Rebbe's team are young Jewish men and women who became close to the Rebbe while studying medicine in the Boston area. They attended our *Shabbatons* and many are now quite religious. One is a surgeon in *Eretz Yisrael,* a *Chassid* who wears a *shtriemel.* Another is a *Chassidishe* trauma specialist in Chicago; another is a pediatrician in Massachusetts. All of these doctors became part of the Rebbe's network.

ROFEH's first director, Laibel Marshall, was busy day and night organizing volunteers, meals and translators, manning the phones and taking patients to and from their treatments in his car (he later became a Professor of Law in Chicago). Of course, that didn't end our own involvement. I remember how, in the early days, I prepared Pesach meals for one patient and took the midnight to 5 a.m. shift as a translator in the hospital for another (what if he needed a doctor in the middle of the night and so on). Today ROFEH has a well-organized staff and lots of volunteers.

As one ROFEH Director put it, "It is an unusual job. You get paid for doing what you should be doing anyway." We all felt it was a great privilege to help the sick and their families. It was a special privilege to help such *Geonim* and *Rebbeim* as the Klausenberger Rebbe, the Lakewood *Rosh Yeshivah*, Rav Schneur Kotler, and יבלח"ט, the Vizhnitzer Rebbe and Rav Kreiswirth, the Chief Rabbi of Antwerp.

At the end of one of our trips to Israel, the Rebbe and I went to the *Kosel* (the Western Wall) to pray. The Rebbe *davened* there with a group of 15 people. Out of the 15, he had helped 13 with medical problems of one kind or another.

The Rebbe and the Steipler Gaon

On another trip the Rebbe and I went to Bnei Brak to visit Rabbi Yaakov Yisroel Kanievsky, the Steipler Gaon. The *Gaon* asked the Rebbe about the work we do through ROFEH. The Rebbe explained how we helped patients locate medical treatment, and I explained how we helped the patients' families with housing and emotional support. The Steipler said, "That is an even greater *chessed,* to help the families cope in that way! You are guaranteed success."

The Steipler was already quite old and had trouble with his feet. He could hardly walk, but he insisted on walking the Rebbe out to the gate. The Rebbe said, "Please don't. It's hard for you to walk. I don't want you to walk with me." The Steipler, however, insisted saying, "I have to walk out a person that does such *chessed*."

Early Disappointments

At first, we helped mostly poor people from Israel who needed advanced medical care. Our patients were supposed to help raise the money to pay for their own hospital bills but, despite all their promises, some patients, even when they had the money, refused to pay. The hospitals were forced to take a loss, and then they would refuse to accept other Israeli patients from us.

For example, the Rebbe once helped an Israeli woman who suffered from severe diabetes. She did not respond well to insulin and the Rebbe helped her get treatment at the Joslin Clinic in Boston. The doctors there designed a special new insulin preparation just for her, and her condition improved. Since she said that she was penniless, the nurses on her floor all chipped in to buy her a year's supply of this special insulin. By the time she left, her hospital bill was astronomical, so I had to ask our friends to contribute money to pay her bill. This was not so easy, because each of our friends already had their own favorite charities and causes.

When I visited this patient for the last time in the hospital, I brought her the money so she could clear her hospital bill when she checked out the next morning. Instead, she kept the money for herself and telephoned me from the airport to tell me so! This experience was quite disappointing. Eventually, I had to raise the money all over again, in order to pay her bill.

Surprisingly, the story doesn't end there. Twenty years later, this very same woman called me to complain that she still had trouble with her diabetes. In fact, she had gone blind as a result of the condition. Now she wanted to go to Johns Hopkins University in Baltimore for treatment. She wanted me to call up a Rabbi in Baltimore and ask him to help her. Despite her past behavior, I called anyway and, when I didn't find him in, I spoke to his son. First, I described the lady's serious medical and financial situation, and then I asked him to help her in Baltimore. Finally I added, based on my own sad experience, "If you have to raise the money to pay her hospital bill yourself, it would be best to pay the hospital directly."

Although most people coming through ROFEH were truthful and honest, after a few more such incidents, ROFEH went out of the "raising-funds-for-hospital-bills" business. We do, however, still help people with free medical referrals; and every so often the Rebbe can even arrange for free medical treatment from doctors he knows.

The Rofeh Building

As more and more families came to stay in our house through ROFEH, things became more than we could handle. For example, cancer patients were often not allowed to eat before their X-rays, CAT scans and medical tests. That meant that they would return very hungry at all odd hours of the day; and we never finished serving meals. When I had to go away for Shabbos, I would prepare all the meals and ask the families of our patients to serve themselves. Although the patients' families were, *Baruch Hashem,* well, they sometimes found it hard to accept such responsibilities, when they felt that they had their own troubles. Another problem was overcrowding. Sometimes we had to pack four children and two grownups into one guest room.

I finally told the Rebbe that it was time to find our ROFEH families their own building, while we continued to share our home with the *meshulachim,* college students and out-of-town guests.

He agreed, so I went house-hunting and soon found a suitable place. My son, Reb Mayer, who knew something about real estate, did the negotiating, and a wealthy friend of ours lent us the money to buy the building. Luckily, its four big apartments could be renovated into eight smaller ones, although that was another big expense. Some of our friends helped by dedicating individual apartments (some are still available for dedication); but we still had to install oil heat, rewire the electricity and find furniture before the ROFEH Building could open its doors to patients and their families. Hundreds of people have, *Baruch Hashem,* been helped and, since medical treatments can last weeks or months, our rent-free apartments can save our patients' families a small fortune.

At first, we occasionally got taken advantage of. Several families stayed ten months; one even stayed two years! Another free guest took ROFEH to court when he was asked to leave after an overly long stay. The judge threw the case out of court, frankly amazed by the *chutzpah* we put up with as a matter of course.

Today, the ROFEH Building normally limits stays to six weeks. We give families all their meals for the first day or two, while they learn to use their kitchenettes and, after that, they are on their own, although we still invite them over for Shabbos and *Yom Tov* meals or whenever they need extra help. When the ROFEH Building is full, we simply take in the overflow as houseguests. All this goes on even when we are in *Eretz Yisrael;* a caretaker runs our "open house" in our absence.

Most people who have stayed in the ROFEH Building have been very gracious; some people, under stress, lash out against the very ones who are trying to help. Health support work can also be difficult in other ways. We live along with our ROFEH families emotionally, identifying with their suffering, depression and grief. It's not easy. However, I often got help from unexpected quarters, I particularly remember one fine lady from Ashkelon who stayed with us for a year while her daughter was being treated for a severe kidney disease at the Deconess Hospital. No matter how difficult her day was at the hospital, she spent hours every evening helping me take care of the other families. The daily *chessed* of this mother, despite her own suffering, was a lesson to us all.

Not All "Cases" Are Cases

One evening I received an urgent telephone call from Israel. A couple was due to arrive in Boston, and the man seemed incurably ill. He had been wounded while on combat duty in the Israeli army, and his hand had been amputated. Later, he developed mysterious recurring sores on his arm and a high fever.

When they arrived I felt intuitively that something about the man's medical history just didn't seem right. Furthermore, he kept repeating that he was the only survivor of a military unit that had fought in the Sinai in the 1973 Yom Kippur War. We helped him become an outpatient at Beth Israel Hospital, where war veterans can receive free treatment. All of a sudden, in the middle of the night, he had a severe attack and had to be hospitalized. The hospital's medical staff soon discovered this poor man's problems were mental, not physical. He was burning his arm with cigarettes, because he had terrible guilt feelings about still being alive, while all the other men in his unit had been killed.

This experience taught us to ask always for a full medical report, in English, so we know exactly what is going on before we let someone into the ROFEH Building. We are caring, but not simple-minded; and we really do try to learn from our experiences.

America Not a Cure-All

Many of the people who come to ROFEH are desperately ill and have an unshakable belief that America is a place where people simply don't die. American medical technology is advanced, but America is not a cure-all by any means.

I had a cousin, a middle-aged woman with breast cancer, who came to America for chemotherapy and hormone treatment. She returned to Israel, but her condition worsened, so she came back to America for more treatments. We knew by then that the cancer had already reached her liver and that nothing would help; all we could do was to make her as comfortable as possible. Her husband, an angelic man, waited on her hand and foot. The doctors gently hinted to her that she had best go home, because they knew she was going to die, but she flatly refused. She was sure that in America there is a cure for everything. Finally she went to a rest home in New York, where she passed away.

She had an elderly father who had contracted throat cancer from years of smoking cigarettes. She insisted that he also come to America for treatment. Although he did get quicker treatment in

America, which helped relieve his pain, he lived only another six months before he too passed away, far away from home.

Curing a Curse

As you can see, we have great respect for modern medicine; but there are still things that medicine can not explain. A young woman from our Boston community — let's call her Chaya — worked as a head nurse and instructor in an Israeli hospital. One of the student nurses she was teaching failed her examinations, but insisted on receiving a diploma anyway. Chaya explained that she couldn't just give a diploma to someone who was not capable of doing the work; and the student left the classroom terribly angry. She came back a few days later to tell Chaya that she had summoned a *minyan* and had her cursed. She was going to die within a year!

Chaya felt hurt, of course, but she tried to make light of the matter. Half a year later, however, she became very ill with Hodgkin's disease (a serious form of cancer). After treatment in Israel, she went into remission and thought that she was all right; but later the illness returned. Chaya came back to Boston, where her parents live, and was treated by the doctors there. After half a year, her illness returned yet again, and her parents came to ask the Rebbe for help. The Rebbe searched through his many *sefarim* and found a way to rid our friend of just such a curse. He assembled a *minyan* and, with Chaya present, the Rebbe and the other men recited her name and certain *pesukim.* Chaya recovered, *Baruch Hashem,* and for the past five years the problem has not returned.

A curse is a very powerful thing. I remember that my grandfather, the Stryzover Zeide, was always careful never to let us say a bad word. In Yiddish, the word *"finster"* means very dark, but it also can be used to mean "a terrible thing." So he told us to use the word *"tinkel,"* a lighter dark, instead. Nothing with a bad meaning should ever leave our lips; because one never knows what harm, psychological or physical, it might do.

NINETEEN

Eretz Yisrael

Eretz Yisrael

Every Jew has an inborn love in his heart for *Eretz Yisrael.* The Rebbe's family had lived there for six generations and although his father was forced to come to America, he had always tried to return. They did return, for a year or so, in 1934, but economic problems forced them back again. While there, the Rebbe learned at Yeshivas Torah V'Yirah in Yerushalayim and his father bought a large piece of land in Shuafat (which was later expropriated, first by the Arabs, and then by the Israelis). In 1946 the Rebbe traveled back to Israel to bring his father's *aron* to his burial plot on *Har HaZeisim.*

When I was a child in Stryzov, and then in Cleveland, I was always fascinated when people talked about *Eretz Yisrael,* about the *Maaras HaMachpelah* (Tomb of the Patriarchs) in Chevron and the *Har HaBayis* (Temple Mount) in Yerushalayim. When I was 12 years old, I dreamt that I heard a *shofar* blowing on the radio. *Mashiach* had come and we were all going to *Eretz Yisrael.* It was wonderful. When I woke up I was happy all day because of my beautiful dream. I also had an "answer" to a question that had always bothered me. How would everyone in the world know when *Mashiach* came? Now I "knew" — by radio!

My First Trip to Israel

The Rebbe and I had always dreamt of settling in *Eretz Yisrael,* and in 1963 we sent our oldest son, Reb Pinchas, to learn in the Ponevez Yeshivah in Bnei Brak. Later that year I made my first trip to *Eretz Yisrael* to visit him. He hadn't been feeling well, and I suspected that he hadn't been eating enough in the *yeshivah.*

On the plane I was so excited that I couldn't sleep all night. When we finally landed and I was walking down the stairs from the airplane, I suddenly thought of my stepfather, the Clevelander Rebbe, and how hard he had tried to come to *Eretz Yisrael.* When he was sick in 1935, he had gone to the mineral water baths in Carlsbad, Czechoslovakia for a cure. He wanted to continue on to *Eretz Yisrael;* but the doctors there said that it would be too much for him. He had returned to America disappointed; but now I had arrived! I felt so happy and privileged.

Reb Pinchas met me at the airport. He had grown so tall. We traveled to many of the holy places together, starting with Yerushalayim. In those days, the Arabs controlled most of the city and Jews were not allowed to go to *Har HaZeisim,* so we went out to Abu Tor to see the *Har HaBayis* from a distance. Reb Pinchas and I got off the train and began to walk up the hill, when we met an old red-bearded man with a horse and wagon. He stopped his horse and asked us in Yiddish who we were. "I don't think you'll know us," I said, "we are from America." When he insisted, I told him, "My son's name is Pinchas Dovid Horowitz, after my father-in-law, who lived here in Yerushalayim 50 years ago." The old man replied, "That's why I asked. I knew your father-in-law, and the boy looks just like him."

A little later a big limousine drove up and some rich American tourists on a "pilgrimage" got out. Their guide started pointing out all the churches and so on. When he saw Reb Pinchas in his Chassidic garb, he told the tourists to turn around and look at us. "Typical Jerusalem natives, " he said; and they began taking photographs of us to remember Jerusalem by. I didn't have the heart to tell them that we were Americans, spoke English and probably lived no more than a six-hour drive from their front door.

I was particularly moved by the old cemetery in Tzfas: the *kever* (grave) of Shem v'Ever — Yaakov *Avinu* had walked here! — the *kever* of Rav Yosef Caro, who wrote the *Shulchan Aruch,* the *kever* of Rav Shlomo Alkabetz, who wrote the "*Lechah Dodi*" we sing every Friday night, and then — the *kever* of the Ari HaKadosh, Rav Yitzchak Luria, the greatest of the Tzfas kabbalists. I had heard so many amazing stories about him at my stepfather's table. Standing by his *kever,* I felt so much *kedushah* that I could barely move. It was an experience that comes only once or twice in a lifetime.

When I got back to America, I found out why the Rebbe had wanted me to take my trip to Israel when I did. The Rebbe, his brother and Rebbetzin Soroh Sashe had to go to Israel for a worldwide Agudath Israel Convention. That meant I would have to stay in Boston to run things. The Rebbe was afraid that I might feel left out, so he had encouraged me to visit Reb Pinchas a few months earlier.

The Six Day War (June 1967), the anxiety at the beginning and the joy at the end, was something that all American Jews, whatever their level of observance, shared. There was a rally on the Boston Common with Senator Kennedy, and then we anxiously listened to our radios day and night. Finally we heard the *shofar* blowing at the *Kosel,* and Jews davening *Minchah* and *Maariv* there once again! The Rebbe and a few close friends went to *Eretz Yisrael* a month or so later. They wanted to walk the streets of old Yerushalayim and pray at the *Kosel* themselves. The Rebbe's mother was ill so I stayed behind; but the Rebbe and I went back in November 1968 for the wedding of a nephew. It was all very moving. After that, the Rebbe and I began going back to Israel every summer.

Har Nof

By 1983 the Rebbe was already planning a Bostoner Community, "Kiryat Boston," in Har Nof, a new suburb near the western entrance to Jerusalem. After the city offered him a *shul* — if he could raise a third of the funds — we moved there ourselves. However, we only stay for spring and summer (*Adar-Elul*). That way we can be with our Boston college students when they need us most, although I must admit that the freezing Boston winters get harder every year.

At first we rented a small apartment on Brand Street. Har Nof was still under construction in those days, and noisy wasn't the word for it! There were piledrivers, tractors, jackhammers and trucks almost everywhere. The Boston *shul* was only half its present size and there were no stores. Trucks came by every day selling milk, eggs, groceries and vegetables.

On Shavuos the Bostoner Shul in Har Nof is decorated with large, elaborate displays of flowers to resemble Har Sinai

Givat Pinchas, the Bostoner Shul, opened for its first Rosh Hashanah services in 1983 (5744); and we arrived the following summer. That first Rosh Hashanah, the Katz family was about the only Bostoner family already living in Har Nof. The Gottliebs and a few other Bostoner families were "imported "from other parts of the city and had to sleep on the floor with friends. Our son, Reb Mayer, was there, as were two of our grandsons, Moshe Shimon and Yisroel Aharon, who were learning at the Tchebiner Yeshivah. Since the *shul's mikveh* wasn't working yet, Reb Mayer and a few others walked to Kfar Shaul and back before *shofar* blowing, while the rest of the tiny but determined congregation waited. Now the Bostoner Shul has a crowded *mikveh* and nine full *minyanim* every day for *Shacharis* alone.

We moved to another rented apartment, right next to the Bostoner Shul, before Pesach of 1986. Although our apartment was convenient, it was small and damp, so we started looking around for a larger place nearby, something high up, airy and sunny. *Baruch Hashem,* we found just the place on the third floor of 23 Rozhin Street, just two buildings away. It has an extra large *mirpesset* (porch) with a marvelous view of the Jerusalem hills; and the Rebbe can see the entrance to the Bostoner Shul from the window of his office. We

Our apartment in Har Nof has a large balcony with a beautiful view of the surrounding Jerusalem hills

have two bedrooms, a nice size dining room and a smaller side room for the women's *tish.* We literally pack people inside for Shabbos and other special occasions; but big events are held at the *shul* or at Reb Mayer's three-story house, a block or so away.

Har Nof is a lovely community, built on the side of a hill (hence its name, "Mountain View"). On Shabbos afternoons the streets are full of young children playing and adults walking to take in the beautiful views of the hills and the fresh Yerushalayim air. Our building is, fortunately, a friendly one, and the Rebbe and I have started holding a special *Kiddush* each year to thank everyone for being such good neighbors. The community, in turn, shows the Rebbe great respect.

The *shul* is always full with classes and *davening* — from 5 a.m. to midnight — and many of the men, wearing black coats and hats, are our own Ph.D. *baalei teshuvah.* Since I've grown older, and now have osteoporosis and a heart condition, walking places and carrying bundles on a bus like everyone else is too much for me. Fortunately, I have lots of old and new friends who help out.

At first we used to make a small *Melaveh Malkah* ourselves on *Motzaei Shabbos.* Then one of our upstairs neighbors started host-

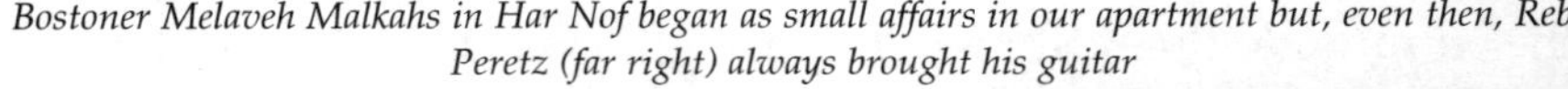

Bostoner Melaveh Malkahs in Har Nof began as small affairs in our apartment but, even then, Reb Peretz (far right) always brought his guitar

ing it. The next year our two upstairs neighbors took turns. Then all of a sudden, everyone wanted to host one. Now the Bostoner community *Melaveh Malkah* is booked weeks in advance, and we take turns visiting the homes of all our *Chassidim*. Wherever we go, it's packed. Reb Peretz Bernstein brings his electric guitar, the Rebbe says *divrei Torah,* and Reb Yisroel tells a *myseh*. There's lots of singing, and it's really a wonderful way to bring everybody together. It reminds me a bit of the Katchkele Club, the Clevelander Rebbe's *Melaveh Malkah* of my childhood days.

A Time for Thanks

Our new community in Har Nof is still growing rapidly, and the *Rebbeim* of *Eretz Yisrael* have accepted the Rebbe as one of their own. He was appointed to Agudath Israel's Council of Torah Sages (*Moetzes*) about six years ago. In Boston, we still have our old home, community and friends; and we often stop over in Switzerland to visit the Bostoner community there. In fact, we now have *Chassidim* almost everywhere, even in Australia. Add to that our children, grandchildren and great-grandchildren *kein ayin hara,* and we have a busy, but happy life. We have, *Baruch Hashem,* a lot to be thankful for.

We recently celebrated the 50th anniversary of our return to reestablish Bostoner *Chassidus* in Boston in 1944. I often think of us getting off that train at South Station, of that young inexperienced couple with their suitcases and their dreams. And I think of all the effort and the work and the late nights — and, yes, the dishes — in between. Was it all worth it? Absolutely!

TWENTY

The Livyasan

A Special Trip

In August 1991, the Rebbe and I decided to visit the holy *kevarim* in Poland and Russia on our way back from Israel to Boston. Reb Mayer and three of our friends came with us; and Danny Wormser and his young son, Moshe Menachem, from Switzerland met us in Warsaw. We had an ambitious itinerary. We wanted to daven at the *kevarim* of the Maggid of Mezritch, the Rebbe Reb Elimelech of Lyzhansk, the Chozeh of Lublin, Rav Zusia of Hanopoli, Rav Naftali Ropshitzer and many other great Chassidic leaders of earlier generations.

We had to take everything with us: kosher bread, cheese, crackers, boxed milk and instant soup from Israel, and *glatt kosher* chicken, fish, vegetables and rice from Switzerland. We even took canned *cholent* and two cases of bottled water! We traveled in a van with a driver, so we could go from place to place quickly.

We started in Warsaw. It was an emotional trip. I was born in Poland, and visited it twice more as a girl, the last time just before the Holocaust. There were hundreds of thousands of Chassidim and religious Jews there. My mother told me how the Jews of Warsaw used to collect candles, *challos* and food for Shabbos in their courtyards, and distribute it to the poor each Friday afternoon. Now there is almost nothing left: just *goyim* dressed in jeans, running from place to place, wanting to look like Americans.

We went to the Gerer *shul* in Warsaw, and then to the home of the Imrei Emes, the third Gerer Rebbe. We even saw the balcony from which he used to address huge crowds of *Chassidim.* His home is now a warehouse, surrounded by old cars and a cracked asphalt street. Nothing was kept up. No one knew about all that greatness or cared. I could have cried. This pretty much set the tone for the entire trip. At the cemetery, near the simple *matzevah* of the Chiddushei HaRim and the Sfas Emes, the first two Gerer Rebbes, the Rebbe *davened* with a *minyan,* mostly *frum* tourists from America.

From there we went to Cracow, the home of the Rama, whose commentary is an essential part of the *Shulchan Aruch* (it adds

The Rebbe (right), Reb Mayer (center) and I at the entrance to the Jewish cemetery in Lublin, the burial place of the Chozeh

Ashkenazi customs to Rav Yosef Caro's Sephardi ones). My father's mother was a descendant of his. At his *kever* I met the Spinker Rebbetzin from Williamsburg. She and I are both great-grandchildren of the Melitzer Rav, the one with the marvelous cane. She told me that, after the war, the Poles wanted to build a post office over the Melitzer Rav's grave, so his remains were moved to Sanz.

Stryzov

From Cracow we traveled on to Stryzov, where I was born and where I spent my early childhood. The Polish countryside was as gorgeous as ever in the bright summer sun; and we passed through a colorful patchwork of fields, rivers and farms. Finally, we arrived at Stryzov, now a typical mix of drab Polish apartment buildings and houses.

Before, there were always people to greet us, kisses and hugs from Bobeh Yehudis, flowers from my cousins. Now we were just an anonymous group of strangers passing through. There are no Jews in Stryzov now. They were all killed in the war. The city is still

A memorial to the murdered Jews of Stryzov, הי"ד

as anti-Semitic as ever — a drunk cursed us out in Polish before we left — but except for that everything had changed. I remembered how, in 1935, the local priest had ordered the farmers not to buy from the Jews, and how he had put church elders outside Jewish shops to make sure that no one ignored his orders. It was a sign of the hatred and destruction to come.

The people in the street looked prosperous. They wore jeans and sweatshirts and drove automobiles — all the Western comforts. Again, I could not fight off the past. I remember the *drushah geshankt* (gift announcements) at the *Yiddishe chassanahs* before the War, "Tanta Bina gives two eiderdown quilts, Fetter Yehudah gives ..." Where were they now, those heirlooms handed down for generations? Who was using my grandmother's linen? Who was wearing my sister's jewelry? What happened to all the wealth of the murdered Jews?

The *bais hachaim* (cemetery) had been vandalized, even though our relatives had paid for a wrought-iron fence to protect it. The grass was high and uncut, broken gravestones were scattered everywhere. I couldn't even find my grandparents' graves. Back in Stryzov I couldn't recognize the town square. It was completely surrounded by stores full of signs and Western merchandise. There was a small park, with a few trees and benches, and fewer people. I couldn't find our old house at all. Nothing looked familiar. I was disoriented. I couldn't put my past and present together in this place.

I was quite broken by the experience. Perhaps somewhere, deep in my heart, I half-expected to see the Stryzov of my childhood: the water pump, the garden full of flowers, the men in their black *kapotes,* the women in their white Shabbos clothes, perhaps even some trace of my grandparents. Seven generations of lifetime effort had built the Jewish community of Stryzov, and it had all been destroyed overnight — just because it was Jewish. Was there nothing left?

The Library

We finally found the *shul,* but it looked so different now from when the Stryzover Zeide stood on the *bimah* and gave his lecture on womanly modesty to three-year-old Raichele

The Rebbe (right) and I at the entrance to the Stryzover Shul of my childhood, now a State Library

and the women of Stryzov. It is now a State Library. Inside, it was quiet. Bookshelves covered the walls on the ground floor and in the balcony. High school students in Western jeans and sweatshirts sat reading or looking into the air. There were no signs of the *aron kodesh* or anything else that would remind one of a *shul.*

The librarians were sympathetic — the educated Poles are more tolerant — and they showed us around. I walked along not knowing what to feel. Everything was so different and, of course, I was different too. I walked upstairs to what used to be the women's balcony. It too was full of books. Then I looked at the ceiling and saw —

An Old Friend

There on the ceiling was the huge whale of my childhood daydreams, circling the whole ceiling of the old synagogue, still swimming in his painted ocean, just as he had so many years ago. I was surprised and overjoyed. He was still there, like the

Livyasan himself, who will swim from Creation until the End of Days, when he will be served at the Feast of the Righteous. He had seen a lot in his day. He had swum high above the peasants mobs and the Nazis and the Communists. None of them could touch him, the symbol of power and faith and Redemption.

"So it's you again, old *Livyasan*! Do you remember me, Raichele? I left you as a young girl, with bangs and a red ribbon in my hair. Now I'm old too. But if only you knew all that I have seen, all that I have done, all the people who still live on in my memory!"

Genealogy

Some Roots of Bostoner Chassidus

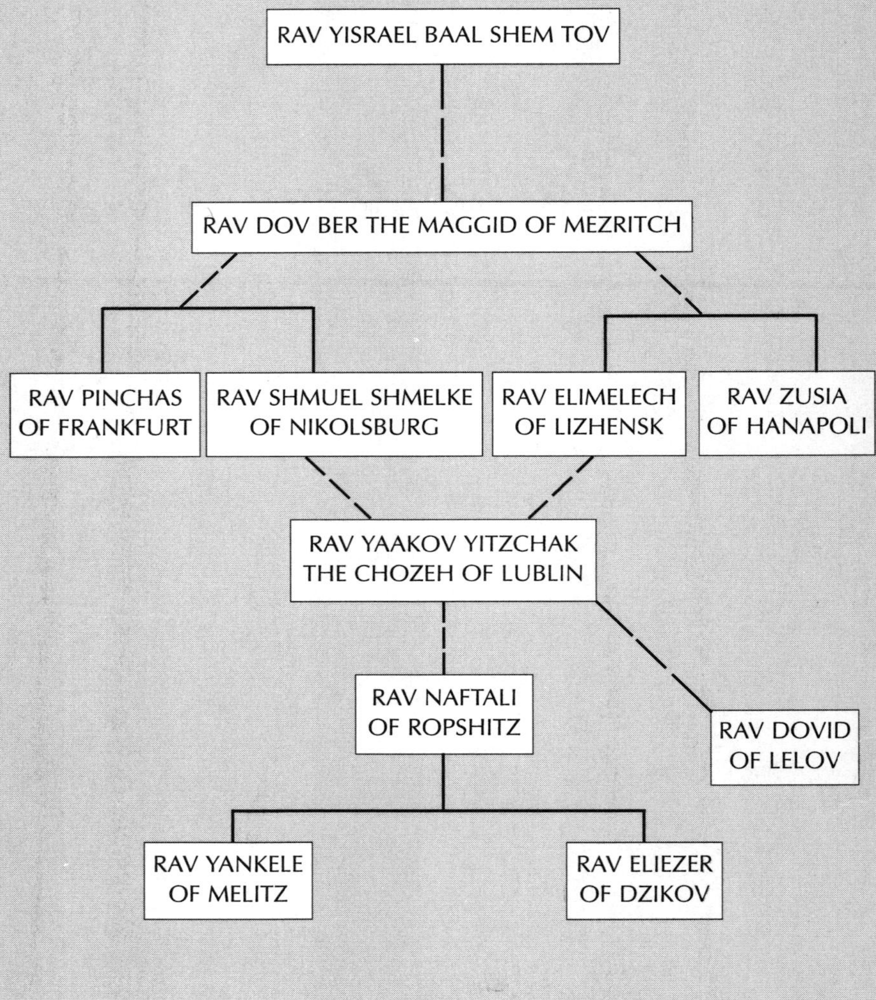

My Family

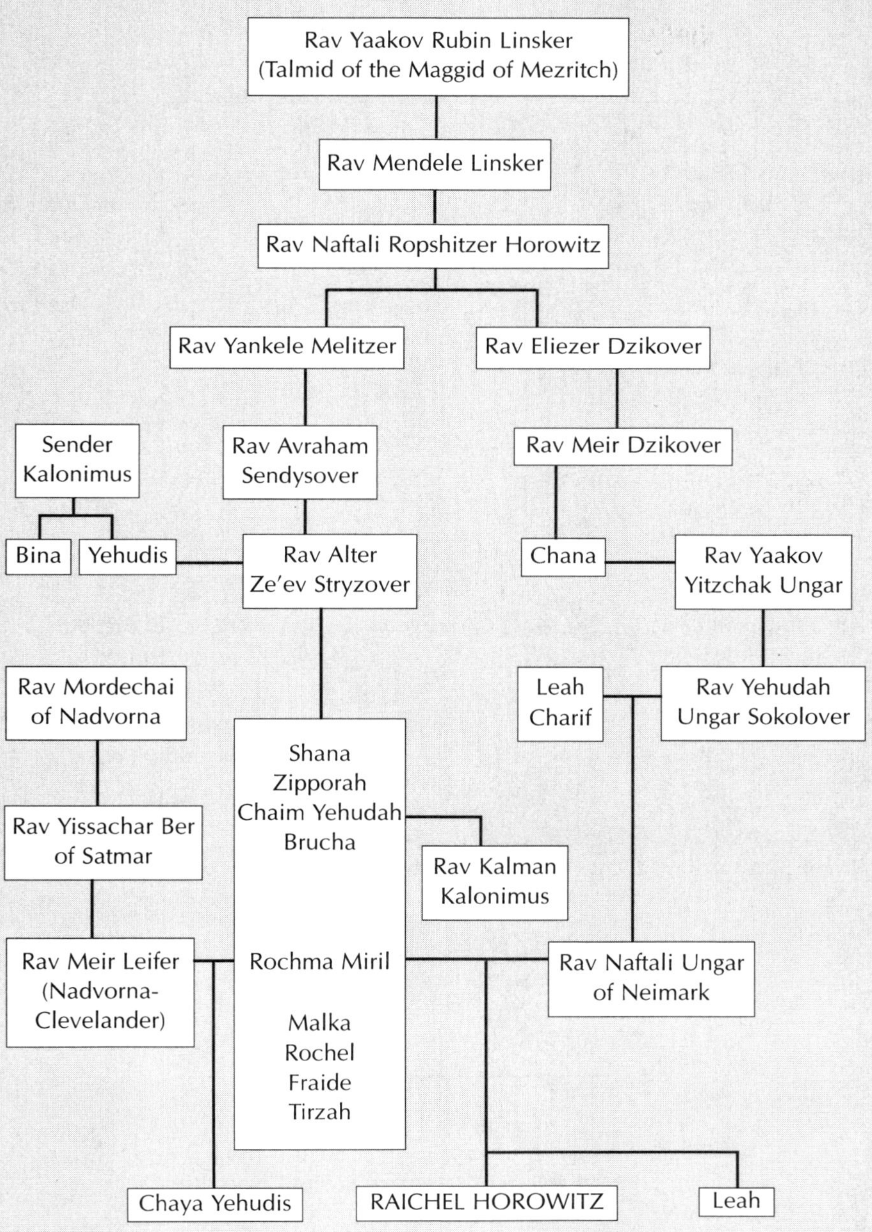

Rav Yaakov Rubin Linsker (Talmid of the Maggid of Mezritch)
Rav Mendele Linsker
Rav Naftali Ropshitzer Horowitz
Rav Yankele Melitzer
Rav Eliezer Dzikover
Sender Kalonimus
Rav Avraham Sendysover
Rav Meir Dzikover
Bina
Yehudis
Rav Alter Ze'ev Stryzover
Chana
Rav Yaakov Yitzchak Ungar
Rav Mordechai of Nadvorna
Leah Charif
Rav Yehudah Ungar Sokolover
Shana
Zipporah
Chaim Yehudah
Brucha
Rav Yissachar Ber of Satmar
Rav Kalman Kalonimus
Rav Meir Leifer (Nadvorna-Clevelander)
Rochma Miril
Rav Naftali Ungar of Neimark
Malka
Rochel
Fraide
Tirzah
Chaya Yehudis
RAICHEL HOROWITZ
Leah

The Rebbe's Family

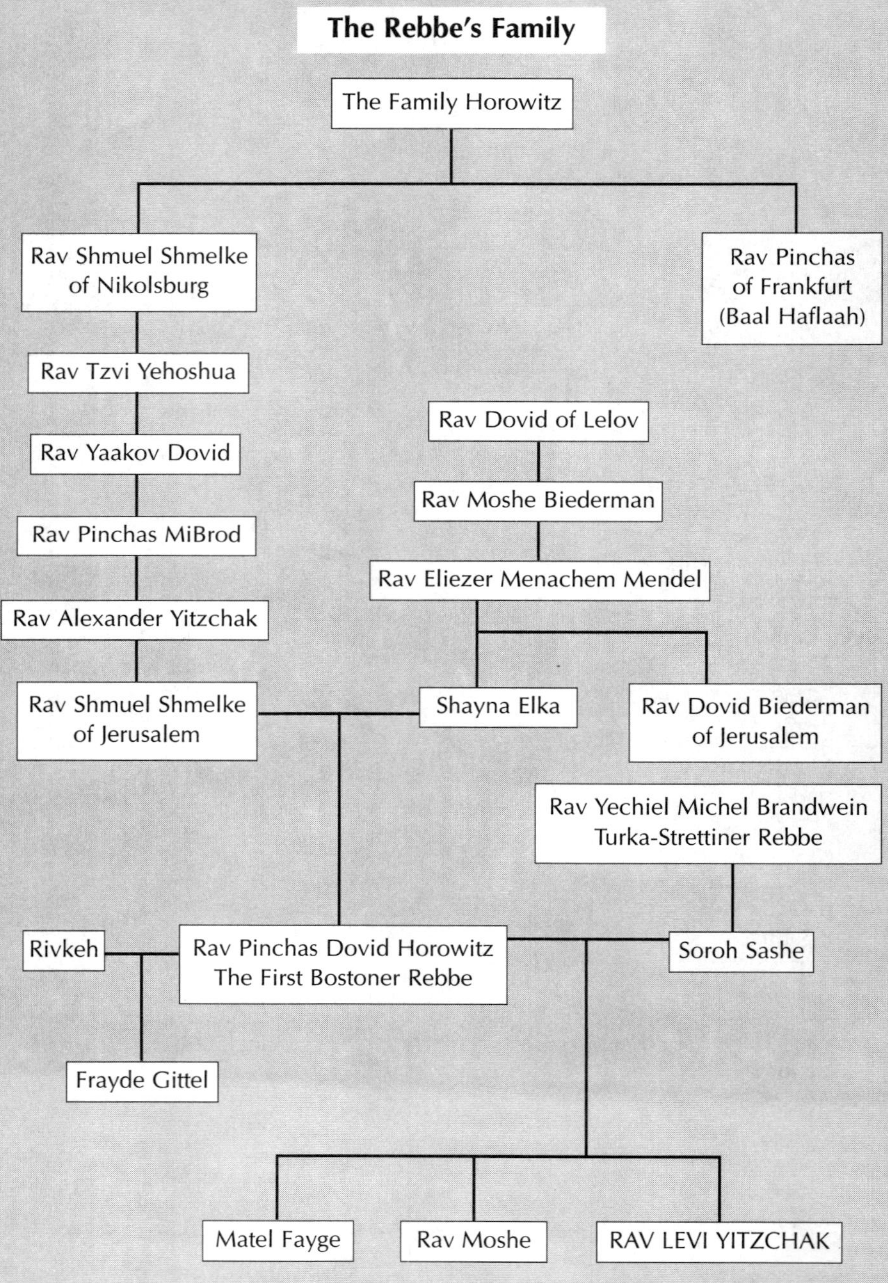

Chronology

Chronology

Rebbetzin Raichel Horowitz, the Bostoner Rebbetzin, was born in Stryzov, Poland, to Rebbetzin Rochma Miril Horowitz and Rav Naftali Ungar. After her divorce, Rochma Miril and her two daughters, Leah and Raichel, lived with her parents, Rav Alter Ze'ev, the Stryzover Rav, and Rebbetzin Yehudis.

1923 — Rochma Miril marries Rav Meir Leifer, and moves with Raichel to America (Cleveland). Leah stays behind.

1929 — The Rebbetzin's (Raichel) first trip back to Poland (with her mother).

1930 — Chaya Yehudis, the Rebbetzin's half sister, is born in Cleveland.

1933 — The family moves to the Williamsburg section of New York City.

1934 — The Rebbetzin's second trip back to Poland.

1936 — Rav Leifer's kidney disease worsens. The family moves to California.

1941 — After Rav Leifer's passing, the family moves back to Williamsburg. With few exceptions, the Rebbetzin's family in Europe perish in the Holocaust.

1942 — The Rebbetzin marries Rav Levi Yitzchak Horowitz, the son of Rav Pinchas Dovid Horowitz, the first Bostoner Rebbe.

1944 — The Rebbe and Rebbetzin leave New York with their newborn son, Reb Pinchas, to reestablish Bostoner *Chassidus* in Boston. The Rebbe is 23; his congregants, 60-95! After a brief stay in the West End they move to Dorchester (61 Columbia Road), where they are soon joined by Rebbetzin Soroh Sashe, the Rebbe's mother, and Mr. Singer.

1949 — The start of the medical support activities that eventually became ROFEH.

1961 — The Rebbe and Rebbetzin move to Brookline (1710 Beacon Street).

1963 — The Rebbe and Rebbetzin hold their first Bostoner Shabbaton, the beginning of a major *kiruv* effort among Boston's college students.

— The Rebbetzin's first trip to *Eretz Yisrael* (to visit Reb Pinchas, then at the Ponovezh Yeshivah).

1973 — Rebbetzin Soroh Sashe passes away.

1976 — Rebbetzin Rochma Miril passes away.

1977 — The Rebbe is appointed to the Presidium of the Agudath Israel of America.

1983 — Givat Pinchas, the Bostoner Shul in the Har Nof suburb of Jerusalem, is dedicated. The Rebbe and Rebbetzin, after many short trips to Israel, move to Har Nof, where they spend six months a year.

1988 — The Rebbe is appointed to the Council of Torah Sages of the Agudath Israel of Israel.

1994 — The Rebbe and Rebbetzin celebrate the 50th anniversary of the reestablishment of Bostoner *Chassidus* in Boston.

Glossary

Glossary

ahavas Yisrael — love for a fellow Jew

aliyah — being called up to the reading of the Torah

amud — prayer stand used by the *chazan*

aron kodesh— synagogue cabinet where Torah scrolls are kept

aufruf — the groom's *aliyah* on the Shabbos before his wedding

aveiros — sins

Avinu — our father

avodah — dedicated service, worship

baal chessed — a person who helps others (f. **baalas chessed**)

baal mofes — miracle worker

baal tefillah — head of prayers in synagogue

baal teshuvah (pl. **baalei teshuvah**) — lit. master of repentance, person who has returned to traditional Jewish observance

baal tzedakah — charitable person

baalabatim — lit. homeowners, head of families

bachur (pl. **bachurim**) — unmarried young man

badchan — official jester at weddings

badeken — veiling the bride's face prior to the *chuppah*

bahnkes — sucking cups used to treat infections

bais hachaim — cemetery

Bais HaMikdash — The Holy Temple

bais medrash — lit. study house, also used for prayer

Bais Yaakov — network of strictly religious Jewish girls' schools

balabusta — capable housewife

Bar Mitzvah — celebration when a boy becomes 13 and assumes adult religious responsibilities

Bar Yochai — song praising R' Shimon bar Yochai, author of the *Zohar*

Baruch Hashem — Thank G-d

batlan — ne'er-do-well, unlucky person

bechor — firstborn son

bechur — Kiddush cup

behamos — cattle

bekeshe (pl. **bekeshes**) — knee-length black coat worn by men

bentch — recite the Grace After Meals

bentch licht — recite the blessings over Sabbath candles

b'ezras Hashem — with G-d's help

bilkes — unbraided round *challah* loaves

bimah — synagogue podium

bobeh — grandmother

brachah (pl. **brachos**) — blessing

bris (pl. **brissim**) — circumcision

challah (pl. **challos**) — braided loaves of bread used at Shabbos and festive meals

chametz — leaven, forbidden on Passover
chas v'shalom — Heaven forbid!
chassan — groom
chassanah — wedding
Chassid (pl. **Chassidim**) — follower of a Chassidic Rebbe
Chassidishe — Chassidic
Chassidism, Chassidus — Jewish religious movement started by R' Yisroel Baal Shem Tov in Eastern Europe in the late 1700s
chazan — cantor; prayer leader, often a professional with a good voice
cheder — grade school teaching Torah to young boys
chessed — kindness
chevra — group, organization, friends
Chevra Kaddisha — volunteer burial society
Chevra Mishnayos — Mishnayos study group
cholent — hot Shabbos stew
cholov Yisrael — Jewish-supervised milk
Chumash (pl. **Chumashim**) — the Five Books of Moses
chuppah — marriage canopy
Churban — lit. destruction, the Holocaust
chutzpah — nerve, arrogance, gall
Daf Yomi — Folio-a-day Talmud study program
daven — pray
dayan — judge
de goldene yoich — the soup that was traditionally the first cooked dish the bride and groom ate together
dinim — Jewish religious laws
drushah geshank — wedding gifts, announcement of these gifts at a wedding (European custom)
dvar Torah (pl. **divrei Torah**) — brief exposition of Torah insights
eidem — son-in-law
eis tzarah — a time of trouble
Eliyahu HaNavi — Elijah the Prophet
Eretz Yisrael — the Land of Israel
erev — eve
esrog (pl. **esrogim**) — citron; one of the four species one is commanded to hold on Succos
ezras nashim — women's section in a synagogue
farfel — small pieces of dried noodle dough
Fetter — Uncle
fleishig — food containing meat (forbidden to be eaten with milk)
frum — religiously observant
gabbai — senior functionary for a Rebbe
galus — exile
gam zu l'tovah — "This too is for the best"
Gan Eden — the Garden of Eden
gaon (pl. **geonim**) — master scholar
gedolim — Torah giants
gelt — money
Gemara — teachings forming the main part of the Talmud
gematrias — explanations based on the numerical values of letters
gemilas chasadim — doing kindness; a free-loan fund
ger tzedek — righteous convert
get — formal Jewish writ of divorce
gevalt — A Yiddish exclamation
glatt — lit. smooth, esp. lungs without adhesions, strictly kosher

goy (pl. **goyim**) — (m.) non-Jew
goyah — (f.) non-Jew
goyish — non-Jewish
groschen — coins of insignificant value; pennies
guilden — coins of moderate value; dollars
guter Yid — lit. good Jew; European nickname for a Rebbe
hachnasas kallah — a charity fund for needy brides
hachnasas orchim — hospitality for travelers
HaKadosh Baruch Hu — The Holy One, Blessed is He
halacha — Jewish law
HaNavi — the Prophet
Har HaBayis — Temple Mount in Jerusalem
Har HaZeisim — Mount of Olives in Jerusalem
Hashem — lit. The Name; G-d
hashgachah — religious supervision (e.g. to ensure that food is kosher)
hashkafah — outlook, world view
hechsher (pl. **hechsheirim**) — kashrus certification
heimishe — homey, comfortable and unpretentious
Hoshana Rabbah — the seventh day of Succos
ilui — genius
Kabbalas Shabbos — Friday evening service welcoming the Shabbos
kadoshim — lit. holy ones; martyrs
kallah — bride
kapote — knee-length black coat worn by men
kasher — to make kosher
kashrus — state of being kosher
katchkele (pl. **katchkelach**)— young duck
kavanah — intent, concentration, mystical devotion
kavod — respect, honor
kedushah — holiness
Kehillah — community
kein ayin hara — lit. no evil eye; said to ward off an evil eye
kest gelt — money from bride's family to support the young couple
kever (pl. **kevarim**) — grave
Kiddush — the benediction over wine on Sabbath and Festivals
kiruv — reaching out to potential *baalei teshuvah*
kochalein — "cook-by-yourself"
kollel — post-marriage Rabbinic study progarm
Kosel — Western Wall of the Temple Mount in Jerusalem
kosher — ritually fit (especially foods)
kugel — pudding (made of noodles, shredded potatoes, etc.)
kvitel (pl. **kvitlach**) — small note, esp. to a Rebbe, stating one's name and request
Lag B'Omer — the 33rd of the 49 days between the first day of Pesach and Shavuos
landsleit — fellow countrymen
lashon hara — disparaging gossip
lein — read from the sefer Torah in shul
levayah — funeral
Litvak — lit. Lithuanian; non-Chassidic Jew
Livyasan — Leviathan, the name of a gigantic fish to be eaten at the feast after the coming of Mashiach
lokshen — noodles

lokshen kugel — noodle pudding
l'shem mitzvah — for the sake of a good deed (lit. commandment)
l'shem Shamayim — for the sake of Heaven
Maaras HaMachpelah — Tomb of the Patriarchs in Hebron
Maariv — evening prayer service
maasim tovim — good deeds
machateniste — the mother of one's daughter- or son-in-law
machetanim — in-laws (father-in-law and mother-in-law)
Maggid — preacher
makah — lit. wound; illness
Malach HaMaves — the Angel of Death
Malchus — majesty
mamzeirus — illegitimacy
mamzer (pl. **mamzeirim;** f. mamzeres) — child born from adultery or incest
Mashiach — Messiah
matzah (pl. **matzos**) — unleavened bread (used on Passover)
matzevah — tombstone
Mazal tov — Good luck
mechadesh — one who proposes a new Torah thought
mechalel Shabbos — desecrating the Sabbath
mechilah — atonement
mechitzah — partition (used to separate the men's and women's sections of a synagogue)
melamed — teacher of young children
Melaveh Malkah — lit. Escorting the Queen; meal after Shabbos
melech — king
menahal — director, principal
menorah — candelabrum, esp. the eight-branched candelabrum used used on Chanukah
meshuggayim — mentally ill people
meshulach (pl. **meshulachim**) — traveling charity collector
mesiras nefesh — dedication, sacrifice
mesivta — yeshivah high-school
meyuchas — descendant of noble family
midos — character traits
mikveh (pl. **mikvaos**) — ritual bath
milchig — dairy; food containing milk (forbidden to be eaten with meat)
Minchah — afternoon prayer service
minyan (pl. **minyanim**) — quorum of ten men, needed for communal prayer
mirpesset — open porch
Mishnayos — authoritative Jewish legal code (circa 200 C.E.)
mishpachos — families
Misnagdishe — non-Chassidic
Misnagid — lit. opponent; non-Chassidic Jew
mitzvah (pl. **mitzvos**) — righteous deed
mohel (pl. **mohelim**) — religious circumciser
Moreh Tzedek — Rabbinic judge
Motzaei Shabbos — Saturday night
muktzah — object forbidden on Shabbos
Mussaf — additional prayer service on Rosh Chodesh, Sabbath and Holidays
mussar — ethical exhortations
myseh (pl. **myses**) — tale or story
nachas — pleasure, especially from children

naddan — dowry
nebach — what a pity!
nefashos — lit. souls; living things
neshamah (pl. **neshamos**) — soul, living thing
neshamah licht — candle lit in memory of a departed relative
niggun (pl. **niggunim**) — melody, with or without words
Noach — a weekly Torah portion from Genesis
Olam Haba — the World to Come
orchim — guests
parnasah — livelihood, income
parshah — weekly Torah portion
parve — "neutral" food, neither milchig nor fleishig
Pesach — Festival of Passover (occurs in Spring)
Pesachdik — kosher for Pesach
pesukim — Biblical verses
peyos — long side-curls worn by Chassidic men
pogrom — mob violence against Jews
poritz — gentile squire
posek (pl. **poskim**) — expert on religious law
Purim — Jewish holiday (occurs in early Spring)
Rabbanim — Rabbis
Rabbanishe — Rabbinic
Rabbanus — Rabbinic position
Rabbiner — Rabbi
rachmanus — mercy
Rav — communal rabbi
Reb — respectable title, followed by first name
Rebbe (pl. **Rebbes, Rebbeim**) — Chassidic rabbi and leader
Rebbeshe — of or pertaining to a Chassidishe Rebbe
Rebbetzin — wife of a Rav or Rebbe
redd — suggest or arrange (a shidduch)
refuah — cure
refuah sheleimah — complete cure
rendlach — coins of great value
Ribono Shel Olam — Master of the World
ROFEH — Bostoner Rebbe's medical support organization
Rosh HaKahal — President of the Jewish community
Rosh Hashanah — Jewish New Year
Rosh Kollel — head of a kollel
Rosh Yeshivah (pl. **Roshei Yeshivos**) — head of a Talmudic Seminary
rozhevilkes — silk overcoats
ruach — spirit, enthusiasm
schnorrers — freeloaders, collectors
seder — festive meal on the first and (outside Israel) second nights of Pesach
sedrah — weekly Torah portion
sefer (pl. **sefarim**) — book
sefer Torah — a Torah scroll handwritten on parchment
segulah — spiritual remedy or aid
semichah — rabbinic ordination
seudah (pl. **seudos**) — festive meal
Shabbaton (pl. **Shabbatonim, Shabbatons**) — special weekend program
Shabbos — the Jewish Sabbath (Friday night/Saturday)
Shabbosdik — appropriate for the Sabbath
Shacharis — morning prayer service
shadchan (pl. **shadchanim**) — matchmaker

shaitel — wig
shaitelmacher — wigmaker
shalom — peace
shalom bayis — matrimonial harmony
Shalosh Seudos — the third Sabbath meal (usually eaten in the late afternoon)
shamash — assistant to a Rebbe or shul, sexton
she'eilos — questions of religious law
shemurah matzah — *matzah* made from wheat guarded since harvest
Sheva Brachos — the seven blessings recited under the marriage canopy for the new bride and groom; week-long celebrations following a wedding
shidduch (pl. **shidduchim**) — match (by extension: meeting a potential mate)
shiksa — non-Jewish woman
shiur (pl. **shiurim**) — class, lecture
shivah — the first week of mourning
shmaltz — meat or chicken fat
Sho'ah — Holocaust
shochet (pl. **shochtim**) — ritual slaughterer
shofar — ram's horn, sounded on Rosh Hashanah
shomer mitzvos — Torah observing, frum
shomer Shabbos — Sabbath observing
shoresh — source
shtetlach — small towns
shtriemlach — flat, round fur-trimmed hats worn by Chassidic men on Shabbos and special occasions
shul — synagogue
Shulchan Aruch — Code of Jewish Law, written by Rav Yosef Caro in the mid 1500s
shver — father-in-law
siddur (pl. **siddurim**) — prayer book
siman — sign, omen
Simchas Beis HaShoeivah — evening festivities during the week of Sukkos
Simchas Torah — Rejoicing of the Law, holiday just after Sukkos
sukkah (pl. **sukkos**) — booth used as a dwelling during Sukkos
sukkos — Festival of Tabernacles (occurs in the Fall)
tahorim — pure ones
tallis (pl. **tallaisim**) — fringed prayershawl
talmid — student
talmid chacham (pl. **talmidei chachamim**) — lit. student of the wise; scholar
tantz — dance
Tatti — Father
techum — of 2,000 amos from a person's residence, the distance which he is permitted to walk on Shabbos and Yom Tov
tefillah — prayer
tefillin — two black leather casings, each of which contains Torah passages written on parchment; the *tefillin shel rosh* are worn on the head; the *tefillin shel yad,* on the arm
Tehillim — Psalms
tenai — condition
tenaim — conditions, especially those relating to marriage
teshuvah — lit. return; repentance
tichel — scarf headcovering

tienes — complaints
tish — lit. table; Chassidic gathering at the Rebbe's meal
Tiveria — Tiberias
Torah — the Five Books of Moses
tzaddik (m.), **tzadekes** (f.) (pl. **tzaddikim, tzidkanios**), — saintly person
tzedakah — charity
T'zenah Ur'enah — Yiddish book of commentaries on the weekly Torah reading
Tzfas — Safed
tzidkus — piety
tzitzis — lit. fringes, a fringed undergarment worn as a mitzvah
tznius — modesty (especially in dress)
tzores — troubles
vachtnacht — the night before the bris, during which one traditionally prepares for the bris with prayer and Torah study
Viduy — confession
vort — word, promise (hence engagement)
yahrzeit — anniversary of death
Yam HaMelech — Dead Sea
yarmulke — skullcap
Yerushalayim — Jerusalem
Yerushalmi — native of Jerusalem
yeshivah bachur — Yeshivah student
yeshivah (pl. **yeshivos**) — school for advanced religious studies
yetzer hara — evil inclination
yichud — a man and woman being secluded together
yichus — familial descent (and reputation)
Yiddin — Jews
Yiddish — Jewish-German dialect widely used in Eastern Europe
Yiddishkeit — Judaism
yimach shemo (pl. **yimach shemam**) — may his name be erased, referring to an evil person
yiras Shamayim — fear of Heaven
Yizkor — memorial service
Yom Tom (pl. **Yomim Tovim**) — holiday
zechus — privilege; merit
zeide — grandfather
zemiros — Sabbath songs
zivug — destined mate

Mesorah Publications, ltd

4401 Second Avenue
Brooklyn, New York 11232
(718) 921-9000